PROFITS AND RATES OF RETURN

by

T.P. HILL

ORGANISATION FOR ECONOMIC CO-OPERATION AND DEVELOPMENT

PARIS 1979

The Organisation for Economic Co-operation and Development (OECD) was set up under a Convention signed in Paris on 14th December 1960, which provides that the OECD shall promote policies designed:

— to achieve the highest sustainable economic growth and employment and a rising standard of living in Member countries, while maintaining financial stability, and thus to contribute to the development of the world economy;
— to contribute to sound economic expansion in Member as well as non-member countries in the process of economic development;
— to contribute to the expansion of world trade on a multilateral, non-discriminatory basis in accordance with international obligations.

The Members of OECD are Australia, Austria, Belgium, Canada, Denmark, Finland, France, the Federal Republic of Germany, Greece, Iceland, Ireland, Italy, Japan, Luxembourg, the Netherlands, New Zealand, Norway, Portugal, Spain, Sweden, Switzerland, Turkey, the United Kingdom and the United States.

*
* *

CONTENTS

PREFACE

In the present economic situation, weakness in investments has become a major concern in many countries. The origin of this weakness is often attributed to a persistant downward trend in profits and rates of return to capital.

In order to be able to check this hypothesis and also to become better acquainted with the growth process and conditions governing income distribution a good measure of these two variables is needed. Attempts to develop this measure have not been lacking at a national level, but it has seemed important to study the problem globally at the international level in conjunction with national statisticians so that experience can be pooled and data more or less brought in line, thus making comparisons and international studies easier.

This book is the work of a consultant, Professor T.P. Hill of the University of East Anglia, England. Although he has widely consulted members of the OECD Secretariat and specialists from Member countries, he assumes complete responsibility for this work.

This work brings to light the complexity of the measures under study, the difficulty in choosing suitable methods for calculation and the relative nature of the significance of the results obtained.

In this field there are two different sources of original information, national accounts and business accounts which are not mutually compatible. A further difficulty springs from the fact that customs and rules for business accounts vary from country to country. Moreover, when the general rise in prices reaches the level observed in some countries in recent years, this detracts considerably from the significance of the results, not to mention the sometimes unexpected effect of the evolution of relative prices. Finally, the evolution of the economic conditions between the moment the investment is made and the successive periods during which it is used, thereby contributing to capital formation, is such that reality can differ significantly from the expectations of the economic agents, consequently making it difficult to estimate capital consumption rigorously and to carry out measures in net terms.

Professor Hill's study is illustrated with tables giving rates of return to capital for seven countries both in gross and net terms. Whether they be for comparisons between countries or over time, these tables do not allow definitive conclusions with respect to the impact of profit levels and changes on economic life.

Professor Hill's study sheds light on many problems, be they the concepts to be adopted, the methods of calculation to be used or the results obtained. It makes a useful and important contribution to the knowledge of an essential phenomenon and opens the way to new research.

ACKNOWLEDGEMENTS

The author wishes to thank members of the Economics and Statistics Department, especially members of the Growth Studies Division and the National Accounts Section, for their valuable comments on earlier drafts. He also wishes to thank the National Accounts Section for preparing under Mr. D.W. Blades supervision the statistical data, which are presented and analysed in chapter 6. Thanks are also due to some experts who gave comments on selected parts of the study. The author however assumes responsibility for any shortcomings or errors which remain.

Chapter 1

INTRODUCTION AND SUMMARY

The subject of this report is the measurement of profits and rates of return on capital. The report is mostly concerned with conceptual and theoretical issues, but in the final chapter statistics are presented and summarised for those OECD countries with data available.

There are two main reasons for undertaking a study of profits and rates of return at this time. The first is that concern has been expressed that profits and rates of return may have been falling in some countries in the 1970's, possibly with adverse effects on levels of industrial investment. The second is that concern has also been expressed about the difficulty of obtaining meaningful and reliable information on these major issues and about the fact that traditional methods of measuring business profits may be quite misleading in periods of price inflation. In several member countries lively debates have been in progress for some years among professional accountants about the need to reform accounting methods in the face of prolonged and substantial increases in prices.

This study is concerned with the measurement of aggregate profits and rates of return for manufacturing industry as a whole or larger industry groups, and not at the level of the individual enterprise. The two questions are obviously inter-related, but the subject matter of this report is strongly influenced by the knowledge that the principal source of data for a study conducted at a macro-economic level has to be the national accounts of the member countries rather than the published accounts of individual companies. It is necessary, therefore, to examine and appraise the concept of profit as it is defined in national accounts, and the whole of chapter 4 is devoted to this. It is also necessary to examine the relationship between the concept of profit as it appears in national accounts and the concept of profit as it is usually defined in business accounts. In so doing, it is impossible to avoid becoming entangled in the current controversies surrounding the measurement of business profits, although this report is not written with the intention of making any major new contribution to these debates. Economists and national accountants have for a very long time advocated, and utilised, the concept of current rather than historic cost for purposes of calculating profits. Their position on this is clear and there is no need whatsoever to modify it as a result of recent high rates of inflation.

Investigations into profits have tended to focus on two questions. The first is the *share* of profits in total factor incomes. It is possible to obtain fairly reliable statistics of this share, and comparisons can easily be made between different periods of time, or between different industries or countries. The distribution of income by factor shares has always been an economic question of major theoretical and practical importance. The *alleged* constancy of factor shares has, for example, become one of the "stylised facts" of much current economic theorising. The second question is, of course, the *rate* of profit, or rate of return, by which is usually meant the ratio of profits to some measure of capital employed. It is the possibility that this rate has declined so much in the last five or ten years as to inhibit investment that has attracted a great deal of attention among economists and others. This statistic, however, is inherently much more difficult to define, estimate and interpret than the share of profits because it requires a measure of capital as well as profits. The measurement of capital, or more precisely the possibility of measuring capital, has been the subject of a controversy among economists in recent years which has been even more heated than the controversy among accountants about the measurement of profit. Given the practical as well as the conceptual difficulties in measuring rates of return, it is tempting to abandon the whole exercise as impossible. Were it not for fact that so many people insist on obtaining information about rates of return and obviously attach such importance to this information, it would be easy to succumb to this temptation. This report, however, does not debate whether or not rates of return should even be calculated but starts from the premise that they are going to be calculated, however reprehensible this may be. The questions to be considered, therefore, are how best to define and measure rates of return at a macro-economic level, bearing in mind the kind of data available in most countries. In other words, what kinds of profit and capital figures ought most appropriately to be entered into the numerators and denominators of ratios which are conventionally labelled as "rates of return"?

Various different measures can be devised according to the precise definition and coverage of the profit and capital figures which are chosen and according to the purposes for which it is intended to use the rates of return. It is not the case that one measure can claim supremacy over all others. Two measures, in particular, are widely used. The first takes a comprehensive measure of profit (before the payment of interest on loan capital) and divides it by an equally comprehensive measure of capital employed (irrespectively of the extent to which this is financed out of loan or equity capital). The second measure takes the profits remaining to the shareholders or owners of the business (after the payment of interest) and divides it by the equity capital. Two versions of the rate of return on equity may be calculated, namely before and after the payment of taxes on profits. While this second measure is undoubtedly extremely important for certain purposes, the data which are needed to calculate it are scarcely ever available at a macro level. Only very exceptionally is it feasible to calculate the rate of return on equity and it simply cannot be used for purposes of a systematic analysis which is intended to embrace a number of different countries, a long span of years and alternative groupings of industries.

On the other hand, comprehensive statistics of total capital employed have become available in increasing quantities in the last few years as statistical offices have accorded higher priority and devoted more resources to their compilation. The method of estimation generally used is the so-called "perpetual inventory method" whereby investments made in previous years are cumulated backwards over the average lifetimes of the capital goods concerned. This method has become feasible as data on gross investment, or gross fixed capital formation, are now available for very long runs of years in the national accounts of many countries. The method has been the subject of a recent OECD study[1] and there is no need therefore to elaborate on it here. The important point is to be clear about the nature of the capital stock figures implied by this particular method of estimation. Capital is implicity defined to be equal to the total value of all expenditures made in the past on the stock of durable and reproducible capital goods still in existence, both machinery and construction, but with all such expenditures revalued at the prices of the current period. Defined in this

1. Michael Ward, *The Measurement of Capital (The Methodology of Capital Stock Estimates in OECD Countries)*, OECD, Paris 1976.

way the capital stock is gross, but it can also be measured net by deducting from the value of each capital good the accumulated depreciation on it, the depreciation also being measured at current prices and not at historic costs. It should be noticed that capital stock estimates based on the perpetual inventory method do not include either land or stocks of non-durable goods held by enterprises.

The rates of return presented in chapter 6 of this report are obtained by dividing comprehensive profit figures (i.e. before the payment of interest) by capital stock figures estimated by the perpetual inventory method. They are therefore essentially *average accounting* rates of return on investment expenditures made in the past, and it is advisable to interpret them in this way. It is also important to understand how these accounting rates of return are related to the *internal* rates of return, or true yields, actually realised on the same investments. Accounting rates of return on investment do not coincide, even on average, with the corresponding internal rates, and the inter-relationship between the two is analysed in depth in chapter 3 below. Most investigations of this question in the past have tended to assume automatically that accounting rates of return must be measured by dividing net profits by net capital, but the alternative clearly exists of dividing gross profits by gross capital. One of the more interesting conclusions of this report is that under a wide range of quite plausible conditions the ratio of gross profits to gross capital tends to provide a much closer approximation to the internal rate of return on investment than the ratio of the corresponding net figures, assuming depreciation is measured in traditional ways. Moreover, the numerical results given in chapter 6 suggest that, in practice, the two rates are not very different from each other at a macro-level anyway. One major advantage of the gross rate of return is that all the problems of measuring depreciation, or capital consumption, not merely for current profits but also for the capital stock, are neatly side-stepped. Moreover, these problems are indeed formidable, both in theory and in practice, and the whole of chapter 2 of this report is devoted to them. The gross accounting rate of return emerges, therefore, as a very serious challengor to the more conventional net rate because of its much greater conceptual simplicity and statistical reliability.

After this general introduction to the contents and objectives of this report, the remainder of this chapter will be devoted to summarising the main arguments and conclusions of each of the following chapters. As already mentioned, chapters 2 to 5 inclusive are concerned with the conceptual or theoretical problems surrounding the measurement of profits and rates of return. The numerical results which cover the period 1955 to 1976 for those Member countries with data available, are contained in chapter 6. Each of the following sub-headings in this chapter refers to the corresponding chapter in the main report.

Depreciation or capital consumption

Chapter 2 is devoted to the measurement of depreciation, or capital consumption as it is called in national accounts. Depreciation is a cost of production which should be deducted along with all other costs before arriving at (net) profits. When profits are calculated net of depreciation, they should be divided by capital stock figures which are similarly net of accumulated depreciation.

It is generally agreed that the proper measure of depreciation is the decline in the value of capital good in question during the period of account. However, since the gradual decline in the value of a capital good is not directly observable, this principle is not easily translated into practice and rules of thumb have had to be devised of which the most common is the straight line method of calculating depreciation whereby the original cost of the capital good is divided equally over the number of accounting periods during which it is expected to use the good.

(For the time being prices will be assumed to be constant, and the effects of changing prices are considered later.) However, if the decline in the value of a capital good is based on the decline from period to period in the present value of the future stream of profits which can be expected from its use in production[2], this decline does not take place at a constant rate but tends to be lowest in the early years of an investment project and highest in the later years. By this criterion, therefore, straight-line depreciation is liable to write off the value of a capital good too fast.

If depreciation is charged on the basis of the decline in the present value of future profits (a procedure which is described as "economic" depreciation in this report) it is shown in chapter 2 that the accounting rate of return is constant for each and every period and equal to the internal rate of return, whatever pattern the sequence of gross profits takes from period to period. When straight-line depreciation is used, however, the accounting net rate of return is likely to exceed the internal rate *on average,* and perhaps by a wide margin. It is not possible to be dogmatic about this, however, because the relationship between the two rates depends on the way in which the profits generated by an individual investment are distributed over the life of the investment project. If they decline significantly from period to period, because of the gradual obsolescence or physical deterioration of the asset, then the average net accounting rate of return based on straight-line depreciation may be quite close to the internal rate. On the other hand, if they decline very slowly, or not at all, then straight-line depreciation will tend to write off the investment too quickly in relation to its future earnings potential and hence lead to average net accounting rates which are much larger than the internal rates actually being earned. On balance, the latter seems more likely than the former, given that profits have to decline quite fast in order for straight-line depreciation to approximate to the decline in the present value of the asset. Of course, it follows that accelerated methods of depreciation are almost bound to write off assets much too quickly and lead to accounting rates of return which are greatly inflated and potentially very misleading.

These conclusions should not be construed as an argument for abandoning the practice of straight-line depreciation (or even accelerated depreciation) especially when economic depreciation is not a feasible alternative. However, they do suggest that great care is needed in interpreting accounting rates of return based on conventional depreciation formulae. When a conventional depreciation formula writes off the value of an asset much faster than the decline in its future earning power, what is actually happening is that only part of the so-called depreciation charge constitutes a real cost of production, or depreciation in the true sense of the word, while the remainder effectively constitutes a transfer to a contingency reserve against the possibility that expected future profits may not materialise. Withholding part of the gross profits earned in the early years of a project because of uncertainty about future profits may be sound, prudent business practice. However, the sums withheld in this way ought not to be treated literally as costs of production, and they ought to be added back to the written down value of the asset in order to get an unbiased measure of the capital employed. It is the failure to do this which leads to accounting rates of return which are liable to be grossly exaggerated, especially when accelerated depreciation methods are used.

2. The present value is defined in the standard way as the sum of the *discounted* future gross profits (or quasi-rents) which may be expected from the use of the capital good.

Because of the high rates of inflation experienced by most countries in recent years, the choice of depreciation formula has tended to become much less important than the valuation method used for the good to which the formula is applied. As depreciation is a measure of the cost of using a capital good within the period of account, the cost incurred is essentially that of using it for one purpose rather than another *at that particular period of time*—in other words, current opportunity cost. Most capital goods can be used to produce a range of different goods or services: for example, existing buildings can be used to house many different processes of production, and so on. A change of use in no way implies change of location or change of ownership. Current opportunity cost can be estimated in practice by taking the appropriate fraction, as given by the depreciation formula, of the current price of a new good of the same kind, a procedure generally known as current cost accounting. This implies revaluing the capital good from one accounting period to the next in proportion to the change in the price of a new good before applying the depreciation formula, a procedure which is easier to enunciate than to implement.

It is convenient for purposes of argument to distinguish changes in relative prices from changes in the general price level. An increase in the *relative* price of a particular kind of capital good increases the cost of continuing to employ a partly used version of that good in its existing use. The real internal rate of return on such a good in its present use is reduced over its remaining life: this is subsequently reflected in higher depreciation charges and hence in reduced net operating surpluses, ceteris paribus. However, the owner of a partly used good cannot be made worse off by an increase in its relative price, and he benefits from a holding gain, or revaluation surplus, when the price rises. Providing, therefore, than the owner of the good and the user of the good, or operator, are one and the same economic unit, the revaluation surplus counterbalances the reduction in the expected future net operating surpluses, so that in effect the economic unit is not really affected by a change in the price of a new good. If, on the other hand, the owner normally hires out the capital good to other economic units to operate, then the owner benefits at the expense of the operators, and can actually realise the revaluation surplus by means of increased hire charges.

The effects of an increase in the general price level are quite different, however, because real rates of return cannot be affected by a general price rise in which all prices increase by the same proportion. It is shown in chapter 2 that if existing partly used capital goods are revalued upwards each period at the same rate as the general inflation, rates of return calculated at the prices of the current period are unaffected by inflation. This assumes that a consistent method of valuation is used throughout so that all other inputs into processes of production, including withdrawals from stocks, are also valued at current prices. (The treatment of stocks forms the subject of chapter 5 below, and it is convenient to consider stocks separately later.) When the price of a capital good increases by more or less than the general average, it can be treated as a relative price change superimposed on the general rate of inflation.

The revaluation of a partly used capital good as a consequence of general inflation generates a revaluation surplus for its owner in the same way as an increase in its relative price. In this case, however, the revaluation surplus is matched by an equal decline in the real purchasing power of the remaining funds still invested in the purchase of that good. If the owner has bought the good out of his own funds, in other words out of equity capital, he is not really any better off because the loss in purchasing power counterbalances the revaluation surplus received. On the other hand, if the owner has bought the good out of funds borrowed from another economic unit, it is the latter who suffers the loss in purchasing power. In this way, there is effectively a transfer of real wealth from the lender to the owner, and quite substantial redistributions of real wealth may occur as a result of inflation. The lender may, or may not, be able to recover some or all of his loss by means of increased interest charges, depending on the terms on which the loan was made and on money interest rates generally.

At the time of writing it is still not customary in most countries to revalue capital goods in response to price changes, and depreciation charges are usually calculated on the basis of the original prices paid for the goods—i.e. at historic costs. As this is also the way in which profits are usually published, this is the way in which they are actually perceived by many observers, especially outsiders. On the other hand, it is difficult to believe that most large corporations do not also practise current cost acounting for purposes of internal management and decision taking, and many are known to do so. It is useful to clarify at this point the distinction between profits at current costs and at historic costs.

Profit at historic costs contains two quite different elements, namely the operating surplus and the revaluation surplus. The latter in turn can notionally be further subdivided into holding gains on fixed capital goods and holding gains on stocks or inventories of non-durable goods. (The treatment of stocks in both national and business acounts is the subject of chapter 5 of this report ; it is immaterial in the present context whether the holding gains arise in respect of capital goods or stocks.) The fundamental difference between an operating surplus and a revaluation surplus is that an operating surplus measures the profit generated by a process of production whereby inputs of goods and services are physically transformed into outputs, whereas a revaluation surplus is the profit received merely by holding a good which remains physically unchanged over a period of time during which its price rises. The operating surplus is the residual out of the increase in value created by some process of production and this can only be measured by valuing all the goods and services involved at the moment of time when they are consumed as inputs or produced as outputs. Otherwise, holding gains are liable to creep in which have nothing to do with the process of production itself. It is inherent in the concept of the operating surplus that it should be measured at current costs. Moreover, it is inherent in the concept of the rate of return obtained from the use of some capital good in production that it should be measured at current costs.

A revaluation surplus is not generated by any process of production by which new goods and services are brought into existence. It follows, therefore, it must originate from the redistribution of existing real wealth, as already suggested. While such redistributions may be very important at the level of the individual enterprise they have much less significance at a macro-economic level where the redistributive effects of inflation (which is responsible for other forms of transfer and not merely revaluation surpluses) are largely self-cancelling.

Profit at current cost, therefore, is essentially the same as the operating surplus, whereas profit at historic cost embraces both the operating surplus and any revaluation surpluses received. Thus, profit at historic cost is the more comprehensive measure and may be preferred for this reason for some purposes. Moreover, because of the practical difficulties involved in revaluing capital goods, the division of profit at historic cost into the operating surplus and revaluation surplus is not easy to implement. When revaluation surpluses were typically only a tiny proportion, such as five or ten per cent, of total profits at historic costs (as was probably the case in most countries until the end of the 1960's) it could be argued that the separation of any revaluation surpluses from the operating surplus was simply not worth the trouble for most enterprises. The situation has, however, changed dramatically in most countries in the 1970's with revaluation surpluses actually accounting for the great bulk of total profits at historic costs in some countries in some years as a result of inflation. Whereas profits at historic costs provide a good approximation to the profits earned on processes of production when inflation is merely creeping at a few per cent per year, they cease to do so when inflation is galloping at ten or twenty per cent. Historic cost profits can be very misleading in those circumstances if they are interpreted in the same way as before.

There is, however, a more fundamental objection to historic accounting in that it is unbalanced by changes in prices. It recognises the increase in the price of a good as a profit but takes no account whatsoever of losses in the real purchasing power of money. Revaluation surpluses are the gains received in the process by which inflation redistributes wealth: somewhere in the economic system equal losses must be incurred, as the real wealth of the community as a whole is neither increased nor decreased by redistributing it amongst its members. In general, the losses are incurred by those economic units who provide the funds out of which the real goods are purchased on which the holding gains are received. When an economic unit buys goods out of its own funds, rather than borrowed funds, it tends to be neither better nor worse off as a result of general inflation. In these circumstances, historic cost accounting by recognising the revaluation surplus and ignoring the loss on invested funds, yields a profit figure which can clearly be seen to be biassed upwards. Moreover, this is also true on aggregate for the economy as a whole because the losses are not recognised whichever economic units bear them.

As already stated, only current cost profits are used in this report: they are, in fact, the operating surpluses as published in national accounts. This implies, therefore, that depreciation is always calculated on capital goods revalued at the prices of the current period, and the depreciation, or capital consumption, shown in national accounts is usually calculated directly from capital stock data estimated by the perpetual inventory method. No use is made of the depreciation figures shown in company accounts. In any case, apart from the fact that the latter are almost invariably based on historic costs, the depreciation which is allowed for taxation purposes has in most countries become a policy instrument used to influence the level and pattern of investment. As a result, the depreciation allowances have usually ceased to bear any resemblance whatsoever to depreciation in the sense of the cost of using the capital goods in question, as they are deliberately and openly manipulated in quite arbitrary ways in the interests of general economic policy. Other things being equal, depreciation at historic cost is less than at current cost during inflation, so that taxable profits are *correspondingly* greater at historic cost. The pressure that this might have been expected to build up in favour of current cost accounting appears in many countries to have been forestalled by arbitrarily increasing the allowances permitted for tax purposes by granting various additional ad hoc allowances, by artificially shortening the lives of assets for tax purposes, and similar devices. The result has been that the actual allowances granted for tax purposes, although nominally based on historic costs, have, at least until recently, actually exceeded those which would have been obtained by a proper, or realistic, calculation of depreciation at current costs (without the various special allowances, of course). Estimates have been made for the United States, for example, which are given in chapter 2 and which show this to have been the case upto 1974, even though the United States has not been nearly so prolific as some other countries in granting various special allowances. It may be surmised that a similar situation obtained in most countries until the explosion of inflation in the early and mid 1970's.

AVERAGE ACCOUNTING RATES OF RETURN

It has already been explained that accounting rates of return coincide with the corresponding internal rates of return only if economic depreciation is used, a method which is quite impractical in most circumstances. The purpose of chapter 3 is to examine by how much accounting rates of return deviate from the internal rates when certain well established and familiar depreciation formulae are used, in particular straight line depreciation. The effects of using accelerated depreciation are also examined, and for this purpose the "sum-of-the-years'-digits" method as practised in the United States is used for illustration because of its analytical convenience. Most of the analysis is conducted on the assumption of constant prices in order to separate out the effects of inflation from the other variables involved, namely the length of life of the investment, the internal rate of return and the rate of growth of investment. In any case, the assumption of constant prices is not nearly so restrictive as it might appear at first sight because the rates of return obtained by the use of current cost accounting are invariant to the general rate of inflation. The actual profits themselves measured at current cost increase with inflation in the same way as any other variable such as wages, but rates of return in which profits are divided by capital stock figures, *both* measured at current prices or costs, are not particularly sensitive to the rate of inflation and would be independent of it if all prices rose at the same rate. If, however, historic cost accounting is used during inflation quite absurd and meaningless rates of return are obtained, as explained in the latter part of chapter 3.

Accounting rates of return are normally measured by dividing net profits by net capital, and this was tacitly assumed in the previous paragraph. This measure will be examined first, although there is the alternative of dividing gross profits by gross capital, a possibility to be considered later.

It is shown first in chapter 3 that net accounting rates of return for individual projects in individual periods are rather erratic unless economic depreciation is used because they tend to rise sharply in the final stages of an investment project by which time capital has been largely written off. It is more useful to proceed directly to aggregate or average rates of return, and the first case considered is that of a balanced set of identical projects which has a new one starting and old one terminating each period. This can be regarded as the special case of zero growth, and the general case in which the rate of investment grows from one period to the next is examined later.

Assuming that a project lasts for n periods the average net accounting rate of return for a balanced set of n projects is obtained by assuming the net accounting profits for all n projects and dividing by the sum of the net, or written down, values of all the n surviving investments made in the past. It is shown in chapter 3 that when straight line depreciation is used the ratio of this average to the internal rate of return on each of the identical projects is an increasing function of both n and r, the internal rate of return itself. In order to obtain numerical values for this ratio it is necessary to make some assumption about the sequence of gross profits (or quasi-rents) generated by the standard investment and for simplicity this is assumed to be constant for each period over the life of the project. (This corresponds to the "one-hoss-shay" case, as it is known in the literature on economic growth.) If, for purposes of argument, there is only a single accounting period so that $n = 1$ and the whole question of calculating depreciation becomes irrelevant, then the average accounting rate of return and the internal rate co-incide, but as the number of periods increases beyond 1 the ratio of the former to the latter gradually increases until in the limit it equals 2 as n tends to infinity. This ratio is also an increasing function of r for a given value of n. These results indicate that the average accounting rate of return always tends to exceed the internal rate in practice, and may be up to twice as large. For these reasons, some economists and accountants have been tempted to conclude that the average accounting rate of return is a quite unsatisfactory measure because it may not even rank different kinds of investment projects correctly in terms of their real profitability. If accelerated depreciation is used the situation is even worse and it is shown in chapter 3 that the average accounting rate of return may be up to three times greater than the internal rate when the sum-of-the-years'-digits formula is employed. Specimen values of the ratio of the average accounting rate of return to the internal rate, based on straight-line depreciation and constant gross profits, are tabulated in Table 3.1 for different combinations of r and n. Although the assumption of constant profits may appear fairly neutral, it can be argued that the typical case is more likely to be one in which profits tend to decline over the life of the investment profit because of obsolescence and increasing maintenance costs. If profits decline, straight-line depreciation will tend to approximate more closely to economic depreciation so that the gap between the average accounting rate and the internal rate may be considerably reduced. For this reason, the ratios shown in Table 3.1 should perhaps be regarded as upper limits rather than as norms.

Furthermore, the ratio of the average accounting to the internal rate of return is also influenced by the rate of growth of investment which has so far been assumed to be zero. In general, the faster the rate of growth from period to period in the amount invested in the standard project, the lower this ratio becomes which suggests that there must be some rate of growth at which the average accounting rate of return is reduced to the internal rate of return. It is shown in chapter 3 that this critical rate of growth is, in fact, the internal rate of return itself, at which point all three rates are equal to each other. Moreover, this is a remarkably general result because it does not require any special assumptions about either the sequence of gross profits or the method of depreciation used, so long as the latter is applied consistently to all projects. This situation arises when an enterprise automatically ploughs back as gross investment the whole of the gross profits it receives each period from the set of projects it operates: in this case, the calculation of depreciation becomes irrelevant to the firm's behaviour and decisions and the firm becomes, in effect, a closed system in which its rate of growth is determined by, and equal to, the internal rate of return on the standard type of investment which it is making each period. This result is related to certain basic theorems in the theory of economic growth. The important conclusion in the present context, however, is that growth is likely to narrow the gap between the average net accounting and internal rates of return, although growth is not usually sufficiently fast to eliminate it altogether.

As already suggested, the ratio of gross profits to the gross capital stock may also be used as a measure of the return on capital and it is worth examining how this ratio is related to the underlying internal rate of return on a balanced set of projects. If the length of life of the standard project is quite short, average depreciation charges are high because the costs of the investment have to be recouped over a small number of periods. For this reason a gross accounting return which ignores depreciation tends to exceed the internal rate by a large margin when n is small, and also if r is small. Specimen values are presented in Table 3.2 assuming a constant sequence of gross profits for comparability with the net accounting rates of return given in Table 3.1. As the number of accounting periods increases, depreciation becomes relatively less important and ratio of the gross accounting return to the internal rate gradually falls. In the limit as n tends to infinity, depreciation tends to zero, and the gross rate of return tends to the internal rate.

Thus, whereas the ratio of the average *net* accounting rate of return to the internal rate tends to increase as n increases (for a given value of r), the ratio of the *gross* to the internal rate of return tends to decrease, and fairly quickly. There must, therefore, be a critical value of n at which they are both equal (for a given value of r). Below this critical value, or switch point, the average *net* accounting rate provides the closer approximation to r, while for values of n in excess of it the *gross* rate of return provides the close approximation. Thus, two regions are defined, in one of which the *net* rate provides the closer approximation while in the other the *gross* rate is the closer, and the boundary between these two regions for different combinations of r and n is given in Table 3.3. When the sequence of gross profits is constant it is shown in chapter 3 that at all points along the boundary the ratio of the accounting rate of return, whether gross or net, to the internal rate is approximately equal to 1.25. As neither accounting rate can fall below the internal rate when profits are constant, the ratio of the *lower* of the two rates to the internal rate must lie between 1 and 1.25, so that choosing the lower of two guarantees a reasonably good approximation to the internal rate. In precisely those circumstances in which the net accounting rate is likely to exceed the internal rate by a wide margin, the gross rate is likely to provide a very close approximation indeed, and vice versa. When profits decline, however, over the life of an investment project, the lower of the two accounting rates may be below the internal rate so that, if profits typically have downward trends, the best strategy would seem to be to take a simple average of the gross and net rates and to use that as an indicator of the internal rate. In any case, it is clear that the valuable additional information provided by the gross rate ought not to be ignored.

The gross accounting rate of return has the enormous practical advantage of obviating completely the need to calculate depreciation both in respect of the current period and all preceding periods. It has, therefore, the same kind of appeal which *Gross* National Product has long exercised over *Net* National Product for economists, but with the additional attraction of circumventing two depreciation estimates, not one. The gross rate is not merely simpler conceptually than the average net rate, but in general it must be much more firmly based statistically. The gross rate of return is also not nearly so sensitive to the rate of growth of investment, and the above conclusions, which strictly apply to a balanced set of projects, do not need to be modified significantly when there is growth. Without wishing to anticipate the empirical results summarised in a later section, it should be noted here that the gross and net rates of return presented in chapter 6 are very similar to each other in practice, both as regards levels and movements over time.

The final part of chapter 3 is concerned with the effects of inflation. As already explained, inflation has little or no effect on rates of return based on current costs, but serious problems arise when historic cost accounting is used. Gross profits based on historic costs are liable to contain substantial revaluation surpluses in respect of stocks of non-durable goods while net profits after deducting depreciation include in addition revaluation surpluses on capital assets. On the other hand, the value of the stock of capital goods held is underestimated by using historic costs. Even worse, the aggregation of past expenditures on capital goods purchased at a whole series of different prices is as meaningless as the addition of expenditures expressed in different currency units such as pounds, francs and dollars. As the numerator of an accounting rate of return based on historic cost includes elements which are not appropriate, while the denominator is liable to be seriously underestimated, the two biasses reinforce each other and can lead to rates of return which can be wildly exaggerated. That is to say, they give a grossly distorted impression of the current rate of return which may be expected from employing the capital goods in question in the processes of production for which they have been acquired. Whether or not revaluation surpluses similar to those received in the past will continue to be received in the future is a capricious factor from the point of view of the individual enterprise because it has no connection with the business on which the enterprise is engaged or the efficiency with which it is carried out. Moreover, it is a factor over which the enterprise has little or no control, depending as it does mainly on the general rate of inflation.

The extent to which the average net accounting rate of return on a balanced or growing set of standard investment projects can be affected by inflation when historic costs are used is analysed systematically in the final part of chapter 3. It is shown that almost any value whatsoever may be obtained for the accounting rate of return, and the figure actually reported in the accounts may give absolutely no indication whatsoever about the size of the real internal rate of return on the underlying investment. It could, for example, be ten times higher than the internal rate and almost any figure is possible. This is a serious matter which brings into question the whole purpose of calculating statistics of this kind. In general, the purpose of compiling any accounts or statistics is to convey useful information, but accounting rates of return based on historic cost do not meet this elementary and fundamental criterion. One of the strongest arguments in favour of retaining historic accounting has been one based on inertia—the argument that historic cost accounting has stood the test of time and is well understood by users. There may be some truth in this so far as the calculation of *profits* at historic costs are concerned. On the other hand, it can be argued that it is impossible for anyone to understand what a rate of return based on historic cost actually means, except in the trivial sense of knowing how it was calculated. It is meaningful only in the sense that adding the UK national product measured in pounds to the US national product measured in dollars produces an objective figure whose accuracy can be independently checked by auditors if necessary. For example, adding expenditures in UK pounds in 1968 to those in 1978 to include in a balance sheet figure is no more meaningful than adding dollars to pounds in 1978 without any currency conversion. Historic cost combined with artificially and arbitrarily accelerated provisions for depreciation produces net "capital" stock figures whose significance is totally obscure, and their use for purposes of calculating rates of return should be abandoned.

Profits in national accounts

Chapter 4 is devoted to the concept of profit as it is defined in national accounts, because any systematic and comprehensive investigation of profits and rates of return at a macro-economic level has to rely mainly on national accounts data. The system of national accounts considered is that of the United Nations[3], generally abbreviated as the SNA. All the data returned by countries to international organisations, including the OECD, are adjusted to conform to SNA definitions. The differences between the concepts used by individual countries in their own accounts and those in the SNA tend to be trivial anyway.

Curiously, the word "profit" does not appear in the SNA, perhaps to avoid confusion with business profits based on historic costs, but the operating surplus plays a key part in the system. A characteristic feature of economic accounting is the desire to maintain a clear distinction between productive activities which create new goods and services and distributive activities which are concerned

3. United Nations, *A System of National Accounts,* Studies in Methods, Series F, No. 2, Rev. 3, New York, 1968.

with the distribution of the incomes generated in the course of production or the redistribution of existing wealth. The operating surplus is the surplus in a production account in which all goods and services are valued at the prices prevailing at that moment of time when they are consumed as inputs or produced as outputs. The importance of the production account in economic accounts has, indeed, been reinforced in recent years by the integration of input-output tables into the framework of national accounts. Input-output tables are, in effect, production accounts for different industries which are systematically inter-related with each other by means of double-entries which enable intermediate flows from one industry to another to be traced out. Input-output tables are widely used for purposes of economic analysis and planning, and an essential feature of such tables is that all items should be valued consistently at one and the same set of prices.

The precise details of the SNA concept of the operating surplus are spelled out in chapter 4. It is evidently not a comprehensive measure of "income" for the individual enterprise: it excludes any income received by the enterprise from the ownership of other assets, whether financial or real, and it also excludes any other transfers received from the state or elsewhere. Moreover, it also obviously excludes any revaluation surpluses or hodling gains accruing or realised within the accounting period. Indeed, revaluation surpluses are ignored altogether in the *current* accounts of the SNA. Given the fundamental distinction between production and distribution referred to above, it can be inferred that if, for purposes of argument, revaluation surpluses were to be included in the current accounts of the SNA they would have to appear in the income or appropriation accounts because they are essentially transfers resulting from inflation. In that case the economic units from which the transfers are made would have to be identified and their losses recorded as well, a procedure whose implications have not been worked out or even considered. Otherwise, the accounts would be incomplete and unbalanced, a criticism which can be levelled at historic cost accounting for recognising the gains from inflation but not the losses. It is for this reason that there is so much confusion about the extent to which revaluation surpluses are distributable. If an economic unit relies entirely on its own funds to purchase stocks of capital and other goods, it incurs losses on those funds as a result of general inflation which are about as large as the holding gains on the goods purchased, and it is therefore in no position to distribute the latter, even if realised. In general, the extent to which revaluation surpluses are distributable must depend on the extent to which they are counterbalanced by losses on funds, a situation which obviously varies from one enterprise to another according to the way in stocks of capital and other goods have been financed (and continue to be financed in the normal case where an enterprise continues in business).

The operating surplus is not affected by whether the capital goods involved in production are financed out loan or equity capital. The distribution of that surplus between bondholders and shareholders is relegated in the SNA to the second stage of accounting concerned with distribution of income generally, so that the payment of interest on loan capital appears as a transfer in the income and appropriation account and not as a cost in the production account. A similar distinction is often made in business accounting. The income and appropriation accounts in the SNA contain all the information needed to calculate the "profit" of an enterprise in a business sense, i.e., including all the transfers paid and received by the enterprises as well as the operating surplus, *except* that revaluation surpluses are not included, as just noted.

If monetary rates of interest were sufficiently high to ensure that real rates of interest were positive (which has *not* generally been the case during recent high levels of inflation) the lenders of funds would claw back as a transfer in the form of increased interest the losses which they experience in the real purchasing power of the funds lent. They would then be no better nor worse off in real terms as a result of inflation. Indeed, if for purposes of argument, the whole of an enterprise's capital were loan capital, the owner of the enterprise would in these circumstances have to pay out the whole of any revaluation surplus resulting from general inflation as a transfer in the form of increased interest, thereby leaving the owner neither better nor worse off. Similarly, the lender breaks even in real terms, as just noted. In practice, therefore, real transfers occur in this situation because monetary interest rates are not high enough. Existing accounting practices do not portray the situation in this way, however, because they do not recognise the loss in the real value of the funds lent by bondholders anymore than they recognise the corresponding losses in the case of funds invested in their businesses by owners. Furthermore, it is worth noting that if monetary rates of interest were sufficiently high always to ensure real rates were positive, the income and appropriation accounts of the SNA would also give an unbalanced result because they do not include the revaluation surpluses which are effectively the sources out of which the higher interest charges are to be met.

The operating surplus, as repeatedly emphasised, represents the surplus generated on processes of production by which new goods and services are produced. It is, therefore, the relevant concept of profit for all enterprises whose principal activity is the production of goods and services, namely all non-financial corporate and quasi-corporate enterprises. The long term viability of such enterprises depends on the efficiency with which they conduct their productive operations. Moreover, these producers are by far the dominant sector of the economy accounting for much the greater part of total employment (including unincorporated producers as well as corporate enterprises). However, the operating surplus is not a particularly useful concept for financial intermediaries who do not produce goods or services in the ordinary sense. As they are principally engaged in distributive activities, special problems arise in the measurement of their profits which are by-passed in this report by confining the domain of study to non-financial corporate and quasi-corporate enterprises.

Stocks and stock appreciation

Chapter 5 is devoted to the treatment of stocks, or inventories, in national accounts, and the way in which this treatment differs from that in business accounts. This is a complicated and technical issue, but one which assumes considerable importance when there is inflation. As already stated, goods and services are valued in the SNA at the prices prevailing at the time when they are consumed as inputs or produced as outputs, irrespectively of whether they are withdrawn from stock or put into stock. For consistency, therefore, withdrawals and additions to stock have similarly to be valued at those same prices. On the other hand, withdrawals from stocks in business accounts are usually valued at their historic costs, the relevant items which are withdrawn being identified by adopting some convention such as FIFO (first-in-first-out) or LIFO (last-in-first-out).

The combination of FIFO with historic cost accounting means that quite substantial revaluation surpluses can be included in gross profits. When the profit figures shown in national accounts are derived from the published accounts of companies it is necessary to deduct such revaluation surpluses before arriving at the corresponding gross operating surpluses, deductions which may be described alternatively as "inventory valuation adjustments" or as "adjustments for stock appreciation". When the national accounts figures are not estimated in this way no such adjustments are needed, but two countries which do work from the published profits of companies are the United States and the United Kingdom. In 1974, the inventory valuation adjustment in the USA was equal to nearly 20 per cent of published gross profits while the corresponding figure for the United Kingdom was no less than 48 per cent.

The use of LIFO means that withdrawals from stock are valued at current prices *except* when stocks are being run down. In practice, therefore, LIFO, even though combined with historic cost accounting, may lead to results which are the same as current cost accounting, at least in respect of stocks or inventories. Strictly, however, the use of LIFO does not eliminate revaluation surpluses: it merely postpones the date when they are recorded which might possibly be indefinitely. If stocks are ultimately run down, revaluation surpluses would begin to be incurred as the items which notionally first went into stock are eventually withdrawn, by which time the cumulative revaluation surpluses on them would have reached very considerable proportions. LIFO appears, therefore, as an uneasy and potentially very unsatisfactory compromise in which the practical necessity for current cost accounting is recognised while lip service continues to be paid to the principle of historic cost accounting. LIFO is actually practised in some countries, whereas in others it is prohibited by law, at least for tax purposes.

The inventory valuation adjustment or stock appreciation is not defined explicitly in national accounts because it represents the difference between the value of changes in stocks as measured in national accounts and the corresponding value as shown in business accounts. It depends, therefore, on business practices which are by no means uniform. If, for example, LIFO were used extensively the size of the adjustment required would presumably be that much less than when FIFO is mostly used. Moreover, as already mentioned, if the operating surpluses shown in the national accounts are not derived from business accounts but estimated in some different way, no adjustment item is needed and hence none will appear in the national accounts. The absence of an inventory valuation adjustment in national accounts should not be interpreted therefore as signifying that there are no revaluation surpluses in respect of inventories in the corresponding business accounts.

When a choice is permitted between LIFO and FIFO, the use of LIFO will generally reduce profits for tax purposes and hence tax liabilities. Companies do not necessarily opt for LIFO for this reason, however, because it is also makes profits appear smaller in comparison with those of other companies who continue to use FIFO. As this may affect stock market prices, the terms on which finance can be raised, incentive schemes linked to profits, etc. company executives may not be very keen to opt for a procedure which reduce taxes by the device of lowering published pre-tax profits as this may be felt to harm the general financial rating of the company and their own prospects. For these kinds of reasons, companies may be reluctant to use any kind of current cost accounting instead of historic cost accounting unless it is made compulsory for all companies.

Profit shares and rates of return in OECD countries

Chapter 6 contains the numerical results for those OECD countries with data available. It was possible to obtain data on both profit shares and rates of return for Canada, the United States, Japan, Germany, Italy, Sweden and the United Kingdom and for profit shares only for Australia, Denmark and the Netherlands.

The objective was not to try to measure profits and rates of return for the economy as a whole but to choose more homogeneous groups of industries.

There is little point in working at the level of total GDP when this includes, for example, items such as government services where profits are deemed to be zero by convention and the ownership of dwellings where wages are zero. Moreover, it is desirable to exclude so far as possible income from self-employment because it cannot be divided satisfactorily between wages and profits. Accordingly, it was decided to aim, in principle, at obtaining data for non-financial corporate and quasi-corporate enterprises as defined in the SNA.

Data on the capital stock are hard to come by, especially sub-divided by institutional sector. It is, however, possible to obtain both profits and capital stock data classified by type of industry, and it was therefore decided to exploit this classification as a basis for disaggregation. Government services were excluded for reasons just given, and also agriculture, distribution and miscellaneous services on the grounds that they contain many small unincorporated enterprises. Financial enterprises were excluded because the operating surplus is not a useful profit measure in their case. By a process of elimination, therefore, it was decided to take mining, manufacturing, public utilities, construction and transport (i.e., divisions 2 to 5 plus 7 of the ISIC) and to use this group which is called "industry plus transport" as a proxy for all non-financial corporate and quasi-corporate enterprises. In addition, it was also decided to examine manufacturing on its own because of its intrinsic importance.

Three variables were utilised: the operating surplus P, value added Y and the capital stock K. Each of these variables was measured both gross and net of capital consumption. Three ratios were defined, namely:

$\frac{P}{K}$ = the rate of return, gross or net

$\frac{P}{Y}$ = the share of profits, gross or net

$\frac{Y}{K}$ = the value added/capital ratio, or capital productivity, gross or net

which are related by the identity

$$\frac{P}{K} \equiv \frac{P}{Y} \cdot \frac{Y}{K}$$

Each of these ratios was calculated for manufacturing and also for industry plus transport for each of the years from 1955 to 1976 (or the latest year possible). Each ratio was also calculated twice, first as a ratio of the two gross variables and second as a ratio of the two net variables so that four sets of data were generated for each country and they are given in Tables 6.1 to 6.4 in chapter 6. The data used were mostly derived from the national accounts published by the various countries after making whatever adjustments were needed to ensure that they were consistent with SNA definitions and the more aggregate data submitted to the OECD and UN. Some of the data used especially on the capital stock, have not been published in the detail needed, and the requisite data were kindly supplied by the statistical offices concerned.

In practice, the gross and net accounting rates given in Tables 6.1 to 6.4 turn out to be quite similar to each other most of the time. This result is not altogether surprising given the theoretical analysis of chapter 3 in which it is shown that gross and net accounting rates of return will tend to yield similar values under a wide range of conditions. It is useful, however, to be able to draw on both sets of data more or less interchangeably, and it is reassuring to find that they corroborate each other, especially since the gross rates do not involve any estimates of depreciation.

In order to condense the great mass of information given in Tables 6.1 to 6.4 into a digestible form exponential trends have been fitted to the data. The main results are summarised in Tables 1.1 and 1.2. The first of these tables shows the profit shares and rates of return to be expected in 1976 according to the fitted trends (not the actual values for 1976 which can, of course, be inspected in Tables 6.1 to 6.4). These trend values have the advantage of drawing on the information for all the years instead of relying on a single year taken in isolation. In order to counter-balance the low rates of profits coming at the end of the period covered by the fitted trends the period was deliberately chosen to start in 1958 when rates of profit were also at a cyclical low.

In manufacturing, trend rates of return in 1976, whether measured gross or net, were highest in the United States and Japan and lowest in the United Kingdom, the ratio between the two extremes being of the order of four to one. The relatively high rate of return in Japan was associated with a high share of profits in value added, but the high rate of return in United States was entirely attributable to very high capital productivity (see Tables 6.5 and 6.6 and the accompanying text in chapter 6). The picture is, however, slightly different for the larger aggregate consisting of all industry plus transport. First, the countries with relatively high rates of return include Germany as well as the United States and Japan. Second, the inter-country differences are reduced somewhat, the highest rates of return being only two or three times greater than the lowest. Profit shares are highest in Japan, Denmark and Germany and lowest in Sweden and the United Kingdom.

The overwhelming impression created by Table 1.2 is of declining profit shares and rates of return. Despite the proliferation of negative coefficients, however, some caution is needed. In particular the evidence for the United States and Japan turns out to be inconclusive on close inspection. There are pronounced cycles in the data for these countries which make the results rather sensitive to the choice of period covered. For this reason, it was decided also to compute trends for the period 1955 to 1973 which excludes the recession of the mid 1970's to see if the results obtained would be consistent with those for the period 1958 to 1976. By and large, confirmation of declining trends in profit shares and rates and return was obtained for the European countries with data available, but not for the United States and Japan. In any case, the negative coefficients for US manufacturing in Table 1.2 are quite trivial and suggest that there is no trend one way or the other in the figures (a conclusion which other studies have reached for US manufacturing). The trends obtained for both periods and for all countries are presented in full in chapter 6.

The two countries (out of those with data available) where the downward trends in profit shares and rates of return are most conspicuous are Germany and the United Kingdom. Thus, the share of net profits in net value added fell from 37 per cent to 16 per cent in manufacturing in Germany between 1955 and 1976, while in the United Kingdom it fell from 30 per cent to 7 per cent. Net rates of return in manufacturing fell from 31 per cent to 11 per cent in Germany between 1955 and 1976 while they fell from 20 per cent to 3 per cent in the United Kingdom. There can be little doubt that the extent of this decline is not fully appreciated by many observers because it is obscured by the continuing practice of calculating profits and rates of return based on historic costs. The distortion in rates of return created by the use of historic costs is particularly serious when inflation accelerates to the rates experienced by the United Kingdom in the mid 1970's.

The evidence is not so clear cut for other European countries as for Germany and the United Kingdom but the data all point in the direction of declining profit shares and rates of return in Europe. With the exception of Canada, however, the data for the non-European OECD countries do not show any significant downward trends. Moreover, there are many European countries for which no data are available so that it is risky to generalise even for European OECD countries from the evidence available. Finally, it must be emphasised that the trends observed relate to the two past decades and there is no justification for blindly assuming that they will continue into the future.

Chapter 6 contains a more detailed description of the various features just summarised. It also examines in a more systematic way the inter-relationships between profit shares, capital productivities and rates of return. The original yearly figures from which the trends have been calculated are given in full in Tables 6.1 to 6.4 and are also shown graphically.

TABLE 1.1 PROFIT SHARES AND RATES OF RETURN
TREND LEVELS IN 1976

Country	Manufacturing				Industry plus transport			
	Profit share P/Y (%)		Rate of return P/K (%)		Profit share P/Y (%)		Rate of return P/K (%)	
	Gross	Net	Gross	Net	Gross	Net	Gross	Net
Canada	32.1	24.7	13.3	15.2	36.4	27.2	9.9	9.9
United States[a]	26.3	20.3	20.9	27.5	30.8	23.2	15.2	16.8
Japan[b]	43.9	32.9	23.1	17.8	42.1	33.6	19.6	13.6
Australia[b]	29.9	22.9	..	..	34.7	29.1	..	..
Denmark[b]	36.7	..	..	..	43.6	..	..	..
Germany	26.9	17.2	12.9	11.7	40.5	35.5	17.6	19.5
Italy[c]	29.3	20.2	8.9	9.8	34.6	28.1	14.3	17.3
Netherlands	33.8	28.1	..	..	35.3	27.4	..	..
Sweden	30.0	22.4	10.9	11.0	27.9	20.9	7.3	5.5
United Kingdom	19.4	11.1	5.8	4.8	27.9	20.4	7.0	5.9

a) The U.S. data for industry plus transport also include distribution and miscellaneous services.
b) The trend levels refer to 1975, the last year with data available.
c) The trend levels refer to 1972, the last year with data available.
.. Not available.

TABLE 1.2 PROFIT SHARES AND RATES OF RETURN
TREND PERCENTAGE RATES OF CHANGE*: 1958-1976

Country	Manufacturing				Industry plus transport			
	Profit share P/Y (%)		Rate of return P/K (%)		Profit share P/Y (%)		Rate of return P/K (%)	
	Gross	Net	Gross	Net	Gross	Net	Gross	Net
Canada	−0.4	−0.8	−1.1	−1.4	−0.1	−0.4	−0.6	−1.1
United States[a]	−0.1	−0.3	−0.4	−0.7	−0.7	−1.1	−1.1	−2.0
Japan[b]	−0.9	−1.7	−1.8	−3.9	−0.8	−1.6	−0.2	−2.4
Australia[b]	−0.5	−0.9	..	..	−0.1	−0.4	..	..
Denmark[b]	−1.5	..	..	..	−0.5	..	..	..
Germany	−2.3	−4.2	−3.1	−4.6	−0.7	−1.1	−1.9	−2.9
Italy[c]	−2.0	−2.5	−1.7	−2.0	−1.8	−2.1	−1.2	−1.8
Netherlands	−1.1	−1.1	..	..	−0.9	−1.3	..	..
Sweden	−0.1	−0.4	−0.6	−0.9	−1.4	−2.9	−2.3	−4.1
United Kingdom	−3.4	−6.2	−5.4	−8.5	−0.6	−2.2	−1.9	−4.1

General note: * These figures show the trend percentage changes from year to year in the share, or rate of return, *not* the number of percentage points by which the share or rate of return changes: for example, a fall from 20 per cent to 19 per cent represents a decline of 5 per cent (i.e. 1/20×100) in the table, *not* 1 per cent.
a) The U.S. data for industry plus transport also include distribution and miscellaneous services.
b) The trends for these countries cover the period 1958 to 1975.
c) The trends for Italy cover the period 1955 to 1972.
.. Not available.

Chapter 2

DEPRECIATION OR CAPITAL CONSUMPTION

INTRODUCTION

There are two distinct sets of problems involved in the measurement of depreciation. The first set consists of determining the principles on which the costs of using some capital good are to be charged against production in a succession of different accounting periods. The second set of problems is attributable to changes in the cost of producing some capital good and the price at which it is sold. General price inflation (or deflation) accentuates the problems created by changes in the prices of individual capital goods, but such problems are always present, even when there is no systematic upward or downward in the general price level.

Although the problems created by price inflation have become prominent in recent years because of unprecedently high rates of inflation, it is necessary to postpone consideration of these problems to the second part of this chapter and begin by examining the measurement of depreciation in a hypothetical world in which all prices are constant. The issues involved are complex enough even when prices do not change. The measurement of depreciation can be construed as one of allocating the costs of using a capital good among different accounting periods. No problem would arise if it were not proposed to draw up accounts for time periods which are shorter than the lifetime of the durable good in question. If the accounts for these periods were consolidated into a single account covering the lifetime of the asset, it would not matter how the depreciation charges were distributed among the different periods, assuming that whatever method is used their total would always equal the cost of the capital good (less any scrap value when applicable). Net profits would also be the same on consolidation for the same reason.

The same conclusion is reached if the accounts for a single accounting period are consolidated over a set of enterprises, or investment projects, of exactly the same kind which are evenly balanced because one project is started and one terminated each period. Provided the same depreciation formula is used for each project, the total depreciation provisions will be the same on aggregate whatever the formula chosen, given that prices are constant. Thus, the choice of depreciation method is much less important on aggregate than it is for the individual enterprise or project, at least so far as aggregate depreciation and net profits are concerned. These aggregates are not invariant to the method of depreciation used, however, if the rate of investment is not constant so that the ages of the investment projects in existence at any moment of time are not evenly distributed, or if different enterprises use different methods.

Depreciation is also used to derive the written down value of a capital good and thus to obtain estimates of the net capital stock. For this purpose, however, the choice of depreciation formula is crucial both at the level of the individual enterprise and on aggregate over many enterprises. The faster the value of a capital good is written down, the lower its value will be on average over its lifetime. Similarly, the faster capital goods are written down in general, the lower their aggregate value will be over many enterprises at any given moment of time. Thus, the choice of depreciation formula has a considerable impact on the valuation of the net capital stock and hence on rates of return calculated as ratios of net profits to net capital stock. (This conclusion also holds when prices are changing, especially if historic rather than current cost accounting is used.) It is against this background that the following discussion of depreciation should be viewed.

DEPRECIATION WITH CONSTANT PRICES

In this section, the major theoretical and conceptual problems surrounding the choice of depreciation formula or method will be examined, retaining the assumption of constant prices throughout. The subsequent section will then consider the additional complications created by changing prices. Two major categories of depreciation are examined. The first is called "economic" depreciation, which consists of the decline in the present value of an asset. The second category is the depreciation which is actually recorded in economic or business accounts.

Economic depreciation

It is generally agreed that depreciation is the decline in the value of a capital good between the beginning and end of an accounting period. This decline is attributable to physical deterioration and to obsolescence, if any. Some of this decline would occur even if the good were not used for production: for example, there may be some physical deterioration which is simply due to the passage of time, irrespective of usage, while obsolescence is also independent of usage. It can be argued that this component of depreciation ought not to be charged as a current cost of production, but as an overhead cost which would be incurred even if the good were to remain completely idle. The depreciation which strictly ought to be charged as a current cost of production is the decline in the value of the good which is attributable to its use for that particular purpose, a decline which will normally be less than the total decline in its value. In this chapter depreciation will be used in its broader, conventional sense to mean the total decline in the value of a good over a period of time. This total embraces both elements, namely the decline which is attributable to actual wear and tear and the decline which is attributable to the mere passage of time irrespective of use.

The practical problem consists of how to measure the decline in value of a capital good over a period of time. In practice, rule of thumb methods may be used but these are not satisfactory without some theoretical justification. From an economic point of view, the value of a capital good in a particular use is measured by the present, or discounted, value of the expected stream of future receipts, likely to be drawn from its utilization over its expected lifetime, so that depreciation is measured by the decrease in this present value between beginning and end of the period. This is the classic economic definition of depreciation as proposed by Hotelling[1]. If the discount rate which is used is the same as the internal rate of return on the initial investment in the capital good, the present value of the good when it starts to be used has to equal its cost, by definition of the internal rate. If, therefore, future receipts are always discounted at the

1. Harold Hotelling: "A general mathematical theory of depreciation", *Journal of the American Statistical Association,* 1925, pp. 340-353.

internal rate of return, their present value gradually declines from the initial cost of the capital good to zero over its economic lifetime (although not necessarily in a monotonic fashion). In this way, the original cost of the capital good can be allocated in a rational, objective way over the successive periods of time in which the good is used.

The receipts which are generated by the use of a capital good in the course of production will be generally described as "gross profits". "Gross profit" is to be understood in the present context as being synonymous with the "gross operating surplus" as defined in economic accounts, such as the SNA. The concept of the gross operating surplus is fully explained in Chapter 4 of this report. To avoid confusion, it should be noted that the operating surplus is a measure of the surplus generated by real processes of production and does not include any income, such as interest, which may be received from the enterprise's ownership of assets. Similarly, any interest payments on funds borrowed to finance the purchase of the capital good are not treated as current costs of production but as appropriations which have to be made out of the operating surplus generated in the course of production. Net profits are defined simply as gross profits less depreciation.

Depreciation as defined above is examined in some detail in the following paragraphs. The mathematics used refer to discrete accounting periods rather than continuous time because accounts are actually drawn up for discrete periods of time.

Let f_i = the gross profit, or gross operating surplus in period i
v_i = the present value of all remaining gross profits at the beginning of period i
r = the internal rate of return used as the discount factor
d_i = depreciation charged in period i
k = the cost of the capital good.

The investment is assumed to take place in period 0 while the profits are earned over the periods 1 to n.

By definition,

$$v_1 = \sum_{i=1}^{n} \left\{ \frac{f_i}{(1+r)^i} \right\} = k \qquad (1)$$

while in the case of subsequent periods

$$v_i = \sum_{x=i}^{n} \left\{ \frac{f_x}{(1+r)^{x-i+1}} \right\} \qquad (2)$$

also

$$v_i = \frac{f_i + v_{i+1}}{1+r} \qquad (3)$$

By definition $$d_i = v_i - v_{i+1} \qquad (4)$$

so that $$d_i = f_i - rv_i \qquad (5)$$

In deriving equation (5) no assumption was made about the sequence of the f's which can follow any pattern: some of the f's could be zero or negative. Equation (5) is quite general, therefore, and several characteristic features of economic depreciation can readily be deduced from it.

First, the accounting rate of return each period, defined as net profits divided by the value of the capital good at the beginning of the period, is constant each period and equal to the internal rate of return when economic depreciation is used. Re-arranging equation (5) we have

$$\frac{f_i - d_i}{v_i} = r \tag{6}$$

No matter what the sequence of gross profits is, therefore, the net accounting rate of return recorded each period is constant when economic depreciation is used. This property is exhibited in Tables 2.1 to 2.3 which contain some simulated illustrative data (which are also used in Chapter 3). Even when gross profits fluctuate from period to period as shown in Table 2.3, the net rate of return remains constant and equal to the internal rate r. In these circumstances, it almost becomes superfluous to construct accounts for individual periods because the internal rate of return stamps itself on each successive period. The converse of this can also be proved, namely that if the net accounting return is constant for every single period over the lifetime of the capital good the return observed must be equal to the internal rate. The proof is given in the Appendix to Chapter 3.

A second point to notice is that economic depreciation tends to increase over the lifetime of the good. The expression rv_i in equation (5) tends to become smaller over the lifetime of the good and it is this figure which is subtracted from f_i to obtain d_i. It must be emphasised that these are only tendencies and there can be exceptions. It is perfectly possible, for example, for v_i to increase over a sequence of accounting periods if the pattern of gross profits is such that large profits are earned in the later periods. An example of this is given in the first part of Table 2.3 where it can be seen that the present value of the remaining sequence of gross profits after 12 periods is actually greater than at the start of the project, and there is no noticeable trend in depreciation which fluctuates from period to period to match the corresponding fluctuations in gross profits and levels of activity. These data also illustrate the important fact that economic depreciation can be negative. It can be seen from equation (5) that d_i is negative whenever rv_i is greater in absolute value than f_i, which may easily happen in practice. Negative depreciation reflects an increase in the value of a project from one period to the next which, as already stated, typically occurs when large gross profits are stacked in the later years of a project.

If the f's themselves are declining from period to period they will tend to eliminate the increasing trend in the d's due to the decreasing trend in the v's. It is interesting, therefore, to examine what sequence of f's is needed in order to make economic depreciation coincide with straight line depreciation. If d_i is constant for every period it must equal $\frac{k}{n}$: thus,

if
$$d_i = \frac{k}{n} = f_i - rv_i \tag{7}$$

then
$$f_i = rv_i + \frac{k}{n} \tag{8}$$

so that f's form a decreasing arithmetic progression falling from an initial value of $\frac{k}{n}(rn+1)$ by a succession of steps equal to $\frac{rk}{n}$ in size to a figure of $\frac{k}{n}(r+1)$ in the last period. An example of such a sequence is given in the second part of Table 2.3 where it can be seen that the f's fall to less than a fifth of their initial level over 20 periods. In general, it seems very unlikely that gross profits will fall fast enough to keep the d's constant (or, *a fortiori*, falling) so that an increasing sequence of d's must be regarded as the normal one resulting from the use of economic depreciation.

A constant flow of gross profits is an important special case which is often described as a "one-hoss shay" technology. The capital good supplies a constant stream of profits right up to the end of its life. Instead of tapering off over time profits suffer a "sudden death" after a certain period of time[2]. Under these conditions, economic depreciation increases very considerably over the duration of the project, as illustrated in Table 2.1 where depreciation in the last period is about 30 times greater than in the first. Conversely, of course, net profits decline markedly over the life of the project, although not by as great a proportion as depreciation increases. By way of contrast, if straight-line depreciation were to be used where

$$d_i = \frac{k}{n} \text{ a constant each period,} \tag{9}$$

net profits would obviously also be constant when gross profits are constant. The sequences of net profits are quite different under the two methods of depreciation, as are also the rates at which the values of the initial capital investment are written down. It is worth examining the implications of these differences in some detail, given that straight-line depreciation is used so extensively by businesses in the real world (and also by economists and statisticians to compile estimates of the capital stock by the perpetual inventory method and to derive estimates of capital consumption therefrom[3]).

As straight-line depreciation usually writes down the value of the initial investment much faster than economic depreciation, the average rate of return over the project as a whole tends to be significantly greater under straight-line than economic depreciation. This average may be computed by summing net profits over the project as a whole (which are the same on aggregate whatever depreciation formula is used) and dividing by the total of the written down values of the investment at the beginning of each period. The relevant totals and average rates of return are given in the final rows of Tables 2.1 to 2.3 for illustration where it can be seen, for example, that the average rate of return when gross profits are constant is 28.6 per cent using straight-line depreciation and 19.4 per cent using economic depreciation. The same results would be obtained by aggregating net profits and capital values over a "balanced" set of investment projects within the same accounting period, and it may be preferable to interpret them in this light. It is customary in macro-economics to calculate rates of return in this way by dividing aggregate net profits by aggregate net capital (as distinct from averaging the individual rates of return for different enterprises).

The difference between the two average rates of return is purely attributable to the different depreciation formulae used, and this phenomenon has to be examined more closely. In order to appreciate all the issues involved it is necessary to bring into the picture the use which is made of the depreciation provisions and the way in which the initial investment is financed, factors which have been ignored up to now.

Two cases will be considered which effectively span the range of possibilities open. In the first case, it is assumed that the enterprise finances the initial

---

2. The behaviour of economic depreciation under these circumstances is examined in detail in Chapter 9 and Appendix III of *A Neo-Classical Theory of Economic Growth* by J.E. Meade. References are also given to earlier work on the same subject by D.G. Champernowne, R.F. Kahn, E.D. Domar and J. Robinson.

3. See, for example, Michael Ward, *The Measurement of Capital,* OECD Paris, 1976, p. 29.

purchase of the capital good by issuing a bond which it redeems on the termination of the project. In the second case, it is assumed that the purchase is made by raising a loan, such as a bank overdraft, and the enterprises uses the successive depreciation provisions to repay the loan by instalments.

Finance by a bond

With this method of finance, interest has to be paid (or should be imputed[4] in the case of equity finance which is equivalent to the enterprise putting up the bond itself) on the full amount of the purchase price of the capital good in each and every period because none of the funds invested are repaid until the end of the project when the bond is redeemed. Conversely, however, the depreciation provisions are retained within the enterprise and remain at its disposal for investment. Sums transferred to the depreciation fund are capable of generating interest receipts over and above the net profits on the original investment project, so that the enterprise's total income will exceed the flow of net profits. As the purpose of the fund is to make it possible to redeem the bond no more should be transferred to it than is necessary, *together with the interest earned on the depreciation fund,* to accumulate by the end of the project to an amount equal to the price of the capital good, which in turn is equal to the value of the bond. Any transfers made in excess of this must be regarded as reflecting deliberate decisions to retain profits for investment elsewhere, perhaps as a precaution in the early stages of a project. Such additional investments must be clearly identified as such and distinguished from the original investment in the capital good.

It is necessary to determine what are the minimum amounts which need to be set aside, or appropriated, each period out of gross profits to accumulate, with interest, just sufficient funds over the life of the project to redeem the bond. This requires a rate of interest to be specified and it will be assumed that the enterprise is able to invest its depreciation provisions elsewhere (either in securities or in other projects) at the internal rate of return on the project itself. The consequences of assuming a lower rate of interest will be considered later. The minimum amounts needed are then simply the differences between the gross profits earned each period and the returns which can be expected each period on the total funds invested in the project, namely (f_i—rk). Suppose these amounts are put aside each period and transferred to the depreciation fund to be invested elsewhere at the internal rate of return: the sum available at the end of the project is given by

$$\sum_{i=1}^{n} (f_i - rk)(1+r)^{n-i} \qquad (10)$$

Now $$\sum f_i (1+r)^{n-i} = (1+r)^n \sum f_i (1+r)^{-i} = k(1+r)^n \qquad (11)$$

and $$\sum rk(1+r)^{n-i} = rk\left\{\frac{(1+r)^n - 1}{r}\right\} = k(1+r)^n - k \qquad (12)$$

so that $$\sum (f_i - rk)(1+r)^{n-i} = k \qquad (13)$$

whatever the sequence of the f's[5].

The corollary of this result is that rk is the amount available each period to meet interest payments on the bond, amongst other possible uses; if that rate is also equal to r the enterprise just breaks even each period after payment of interest of the bond.

4. See Nancy Ruggles and Richard Ruggles, *The Design of Economic Accounts,* National Bureau of Economic Research, General Series No. 89, Columbia Univ. Press, 1970, pp. 101, 102.

5. See J.E. Meade, *op. cit.,* pp. 81-84, for a further discussion of this point in the special case where the f's are all constant, the "one-hoss-shay" case.

Where the initial funds are raised out of equity capital r can also be interpreted as the rate of interest (=rate of profit) on the amount of equity capital invested. Of course, given that the funds invested in the project equal k throughout (until the bond is redeemed) it can be argued that rk *ought* to become available each period (irrespective of the sequence of the f's) because of the definition of r, the internal rate of return[6]. It should be noticed, however, that just as the transfer to the depreciation fund, namely (f_i—rk), is not the same as the depreciation provision itself, namely (f_i—rv_i) the enterprise's net income, namely rk, is not equal to net profits, namely rv_i. The depreciation provision is equal to (f_i—rk) *plus* the interest earned each period on the depreciation fund accumulated up to the beginning of each period, the sum of the two components being identical with economic depreciation as defined in (4) above. Similarly, the enterprise's net income is equal to net profits *plus* the interest received on the depreciation fund.

The decomposition of the depreciation provision into the transfer from profits and the interest on accumulated depreciation fund is illustrated in Table 2.1 under the general heading of "Finance by a bond". The transfer from profits is, of course, constant when gross profits are constant, and amounts to only 2.9 per cent of gross profits in the case illustrated. The interest component grows from zero in the first period to an amount equal to 80.9 per cent of gross profits in the twentieth period, or roughly 30 times the transfer element. In general, when both r and n are large, it is to be expected that the interest component will dwarf the transfer element in the later years of a project.

In the case of straight-line depreciation, the amount transferred to the depreciation fund in the first period is equal to $\frac{k}{n}$. This earns interest equal to $\frac{rk}{n}$ in the second period (assuming for purposes of comparability that amounts held in the depreciation fund continue to be invested at a rate of interest equal to r) so that only $\frac{k}{n}(1 - r)$ needs to be transferred out of gross profits in the second period. Similarly, interest of $\frac{2rk}{n}$ is earned in the third period so that only $\frac{k}{n}(1 - 2r)$ needs to be transferred, and so on in subsequent periods. After $(1+\frac{1}{r})$ periods no further transfers need to be made out of gross profits as the interest on the accumulated fund is more than sufficient to provide for depreciation on its own. Beyond this point net profits plus the interest earned on the depreciation actually exceed gross profits by growing amounts. This is illustrated in Table 2.2 under the heading "Finance by a bond" where the net income of the enterprise exceeds gross profits after the sixth period.

When straight-line depreciation is used the total interest earned on the depreciation fund over the life of the project greatly exceeds that when economic depreciation is used because the build up of the fund is much more rapid in the early periods. Straight-line depreciation is, in effect, a form of "accelerated" depreciation in comparison with economic depreciation, although the term "accelerated depreciation" is normally used to refer to depreciation methods which have an even more rapid build up in the early periods. Because the total

6. If f_i happens to be less than rk in any period, it is tacitly assumed that the difference can be borrowed, possibly out of the depreciation fund itself, at an interest rate equal to r.

interest earned over the project is greater for straight-line than economic depreciation, total net income is also greater. When the *average* net income per period is divided by the amount of the initial investment, namely k, the resulting figure is identical with the internal rate of return when economic depreciation is used; for example, 97.1 divided by 500 in Table 2.1. However, with straight-line depreciation this ratio is significantly greater than r (even on the assumption that the interest earned on depreciation is no more than r); thus, in Table 2.2 the ratio is 0.242, or 121.1 divided by 500. This accounting legerdemain is accomplished even though internal rate of return, the rate of interest earned on the depreciation fund and the size of the initial investment are exactly the same in both cases. The higher total net income is the substance behind the illusion of higher average accounting rates of return based on straight-line depreciation.

While the total net income earned over the life of the project can indeed be genuinely increased by accelerating depreciation, it should also be clear that the rate of return on investment *cannot* be increased by this manœuvre, given that, by assumption, the only investment opportunities open to the enterprise yield the internal rate of return. It follows, therefore, that the division of average net income by the amount of the initial investment is not generally a proper measure of the rate of return. The correct measure of capital at any moment of time is given by the sum of the present value of the remaining sequence of gross profits earned by using the capital good plus the accumulated depreciation fund. This is what the project would be worth if it were to be sold sometime during the life of the project. Now, the only circumstances in which the sum of the present value plus accumulated depreciation is always identical with the amount of the initial investment is when economic depreciation is used. When straight-line depreciation is used the sum of the two exceeds the initial investment after the first period precisely because straight-line depreciation is accelerated in comparison with economic depreciation. The sum of the present value plus accumulated depreciation will be called the "total" investment at any moment of time, to distinguish it from the initial investment in the capital good. When economic depreciation is used the value of the total investment must coincide with that of the initial investment because of the way in which economic depreciation is defined, but with straight-line depreciation the total investment tends to increase during the early periods reaching a peak somewhere in the second half of the project. It subsequently declines towards the amount of the initial investment because in the later stages straight-line depreciation is less than economic depreciation. On average, therefore, the total investment tends to exceed the initial investment over the project as a whole. The average net income should be divided by average value of the *total* investment per period in order to get a proper measure of the enterprise's rate of return. When this is done, it always coincides with the internal rate of return (assuming that the interest earned on the depreciation fund also equals the internal rate) whatever the depreciation method used. It is a measure which is invariant to the accounting procedures adopted.

The behaviour of total investment when straight-line depreciation is used is illustrated in Table 2.2. It reaches a peak two-thirds of the way through the project at which time it is about 38 per cent higher than the initial investment, and it is about 25 per cent higher on average over the total life of the project. The division of average net income per period, namely 121.1 by the average total investment per period, namely 623.7, yields the internal rate of return of 19.42 per cent. The analogous ratio in Table 2.1 where economic depreciation is used is 97.12 divided by 500: in this case, both the net income and the total investment are constant each period, and the ratio of one to the other yields the internal rate of return period by period. Table 2.2 also shows the net investment made each period as a consequence of the provision for depreciation diverging from the decline in the value of the project: the amount of net investment undertaken each period is given by the formula

$$\frac{k}{n}(f_i - rv_i) \tag{14}$$

when straight-line depreciation is used. This expression tends to be positive until the later periods of the project when v_i becomes small. It sums identically to zero over the total life of the project.

The division of average net income by the initial investment alone is a "bogus" rate of return because it ignores the investment (or disinvestment) which is taking place continuously throughout the project whenever the provision for depreciation differs from the decline in the value of the capital good. It might appear that such a return would never be calculated, but in fact it is commonly calculated in a slightly different form. Suppose that both the depreciation fund and the income received from it are omitted from the calculation: the rate of return is then calculated on the project alone by dividing average net profits per period by the average depreciated value of the capital good in each period. This is also a "bogus" measure of the rate of return on investment unless economic depreciation is used, because the written down value of the capital good is incomplete as a measure of the capital invested. It is necessary to add back to it the amount by which accumulated depreciation exceeds the decline in the value of the capital good, which, in effect, constitutes a contingency reserve held against the possibility of future gross profits not being realised in full. When estimates of net capital are obtained from business or economic accounts which have been compiled using straight-line depreciation, this amount is not added back, in practice, so that the rates of return calculated are liable to be bogus and biassed upwards as measures of rates of return on investment. For example, the rate of return calculated in this way for the data in Table 2.2 is 75 divided by 262.5, or 28.6 per cent, which bears little relation to the internal rate of return of 19.4 per cent[7].

In practice, the estimates of net capital stock which are used in Chapter 6 of this report are built up by assuming that depreciation is linear. The rates of return calculated by dividing net profits by net capital presumably are subject to the kind of upward bias discussed here. It is important, therefore, to obtain an impression of the orders of magnitude involved which depend primarily on the size of the internal rate of return and the number of periods in the life of the project. These questions are explored in some detail in the next chapter, where it is also shown that when r or n are large, the ratio of gross profits to the gross capital stock is likely to provide a closer approximation to the internal rate of return than the ratio of the two net figures.

Returning to the example under consideration, the correct description of the situation in which straight-line depreciation is used is that a fraction of net profits (i.e. gross profits less economic depreciation) is being transferred each period to a contingency reserve and re-invested. The fraction transferred in this way is higher in the early periods eventually becoming negative in the final periods. Now, this may be sound, prudent business practice in the face of uncertainty, but it should not be allowed to confuse the measurement of rates of return on investment. The excess of straight-line over economic depreciation is strictly an appropriation

7. In order to obtain a figure of 28.6 per cent for average net income divided by the initial investment it would be necessary to assume that depreciation provisions could be invested at a rate of interest of 28.6 per cent. This is an absurd assumption not merely because the figure of 28.6 per cent is merely an accounting artefact but also because it would make the investment of depreciation much more profitable than the original investment itself (which would presumably never be undertaken therefore).

out of net profits as distinct from a charge against gross profits. It should not be labelled "depreciation", even though it is conventionally treated as such, because classifying it as depreciation distorts the measurement of capital employed and hences rates of return.

It is easy to see why straight-line depreciation is preferred to economic depreciation in practice. Obviously, it is extremely difficult, if not impossible, to make a precise and reliable estimate of economic depreciation when future profits are uncertain. The use of the straight-line method, however, changes the time profile of net profits in such a way as to reduce their present value by postponing the receipt of some net profits from early to later periods. Although this may be justified on grounds of uncertainty about future profits, the loss involved is also compensated to some extent by the increase in the present value of the interest which may be expected from the higher provisions for depreciation made during the early years. These reasons may be re-inforced by a third factor, in practice, namely the taxation of profits. To the extent that the depreciation chargeable for tax purposes may be accelerated, the present value of the stream of taxes levied on profits is also reduced.

The point at issue is not, therefore, the amount to be set aside out of gross profits and transferred to a reserve which may be used, amongst other things, to provide funds which can be used to redeem the bond on the termination of the project. It would either be an extremely confident or foolhardy enterprise that set aside as little as economic depreciation in the early years of a project given the inevitable uncertainty about future profits. However, it is objectionable to call such transfers "depreciation" when it may be surmised that they greatly exceed the amounts needed for this purpose in the early periods of a project. If it is accepted that depreciation measures the decline in the value of the capital good used in production, it must also be accepted that depreciation *cannot* be accelerated. There is only one figure for the depreciation incurred in any accounting period, and it cannot be manipulated to suit the convenience of the enterprise. It is possible to transfer to reserve an amount greater than this, but is must not be labelled "depreciation" and thereby distort the measures of net profits, net capital and rates of return.

Before leaving the case in which the enterprise is assumed to raise the finance by a bond redeemed on the project's termination, it is necessary to examine what happens when the enterprise is unable to invest its depreciation provisions at the internal rate of return and is forced to accept a lower rate of interest. In practice, this must be regarded as the norm rather than the exception, given that the original investment in the project may be presumed to have been profitable. It must be emphasised, however, that the investment of depreciation provisions is quite a separate matter from the calculation of depreciation itself, and neither economic nor straight-line depreciation can be affected by the interest earned on the depreciation fund. (There may not even be such a fund if depreciation provisions are used to repay a loan instead of being retained.) On the other hand, the amounts which need to be transferred out of gross profits into the depreciation fund (which must never be confused with the depreciation charges themselves) are inevitably increased if the rate of interest which can be earned on the depreciation fund is reduced. The transfers needed are increased both for economic and straight-line depreciation, or indeed for any depreciation method whatsoever. In short, the enterprise's average net income is reduced whatever depreciation method is used.

The numerical illustrations shown in Tables 2.1 and 2.2 assume constant sequences of gross profits. If, however, declining sequences of profits were used for purposes of illustration, the differences between economic and straight-line depreciation would be reduced, and could, theoretically, disappear altogether if the sequences of profits happened to conform to equation (8) above. Thus, while Tables 2.1 and 2.2 throw into sharp relief the consequences for average accounting rates of return of using straight-line rather than economic depreciation, it is not being suggested that the differences are typically as great as these data indicate. In general, the faster the gross profits tend to decline over the life of an individual investment project, the less likely it is that straight-line depreciation will tend to write off the value of the asset too quickly and lead to exaggerated accounting rates of return. Only when profits do not have downward trends is it certain that straight-line depreciation is *de facto* accelerated.

Suppose in the examples used above the interest which can be earned on the depreciation fund is only 10 per cent, compared with an internal rate of return of 19.4 per cent. In order to accumulate 500 over 20 periods 8.73 needs to be invested at 10 per cent each period, and this amount would have to be transferred each period instead of the 2.87 when interest earned is 19.4 per cent. When economic depreciation is used, therefore, the net income of the enterprise is reduced by 5.86 per period, and the return which is earned on the total investment falls to 18.25 per cent. The internal rate of return is still earned on the original project but not on the total investment.

When straight-line depreciation is used the return on the total investment is also reduced but to an even greater extent because a larger share of the total investment is locked up in accumulated depreciation provisions. In the example illustrated in Table 2.2 the total interest earned is cut from 922.5 to 475 if the rate of interest is cut from 19.4 per cent to 10 per cent, so that the true return on the total investment is cut from 19.4 per cent to 15.8 per cent, while the bogus return calculated on the value of the initial investment alone falls from 24.2 per cent to 19.8 per cent. In general, it may be inferred that the more accelerated the depreciation method is the greater the relative loss which is incurred as a result of lower interest rates on the depreciation fund.

Whether economic or straight-line depreciation is used, greater amounts have to be transferred out of gross profits over the life of the project to compensate for the lower interest earned on the depreciation fund, thereby reducing the net income of the enterprise on aggregate. However, lower interest rates may also reduce the rate of interest paid on the bond which the enterprise itself issued to finance the project. As interest is paid on the full amount of the bond throughout the project, the interest paid must always exceed the interest received on the depreciation fund if both rates are the same so that the enterprise always gains from a reduction in interest rates. However, this must not be allowed to obscure the further point that the attractiveness of straight-line, or even more accelerated methods of depreciation, is reduced vis-a-vis economic depreciation the greater the gap between the internal rate of return on the project itself and the rate of interest, or more generally the rate of return, which can be earned on accumulated depreciation provisions. The sacrifice incurred by postponing the receipt of net profits becomes more costly as the return which may be earned on depreciation is reduced.

Finance by loan

It is necessary to examine to what extent, if any, the above conclusions needed to be modified if the financial arrangements are such that the capital good is purchased by a loan which is gradually paid off by instalments out of sums put aside for depreciation. In this case, there is no depreciation fund so that the yield available on accumulated depreciation is irrelevant. Net income and net profits coincide as no additional interest is earned. The capital invested in the project is gradually reduced to zero over the life of the project.

Once again the important factor is the effect of the depreciation method on the valuation of the capital invested in the project, rather than on the measurement of net profits. As already stated, over the complete life of a project (or alternatively, on aggregate over a balanced set of projects) net profits are the same whatever the depreciation method used. On the other hand, the effects on the value of capital are not self-cancelling, on aggregate or on average.

If the amount of depreciation charged in any period, and hence the amount of the loan repaid, is equal to economic depreciation, the decline in the value of capital is equal to the reduction in the loan. However, if straight-line depreciation is used, the reduction in the loan will normally exceed the decline in the value of the capital good, perhaps by a considerable amount. As the reduction of a liability is formally equivalent to an increase in asset, it must be concluded that, on balance, the enterprise has injected some additional capital into the project. In effect, the enterprise has substituted some of its own equity capital for the loan by repaying the loan faster than is required by the decline in value of the capital good. The good continues to be predominantly financed by the loan, but on the margin a steadily increasing proportion of the finance is tacitly being provided by appropriations out of net profits. This element is missing from the balance sheet, and is counterbalanced by the fact that the written down value of the capital good based on straight-line depreciation (or *a fortiori,* on even more accelerated forms of depreciation) tends consistently to understate its present value after the first period. Thus, rates of return based on these written down values are biassed upwards, both in particular periods and on average over the project. The argument is essentially the same as that used in the previous section and need not be elaborated at length.

The wisdom of withholding parts of net profits and appropriating them for purposes of accelerating the repayment of the enterprise's debt is not at issue. This is a matter of judgement in the light of the actual situation in which the enterprise finds itself. However, such appropriations must be recognised for what they are, and not treated as current costs which are chargeable against gross profits.

The enterprise also benefits by reducing the interest charges on the loan faster than would be the case if repayments were made at a rate equal to economic depreciation. If, for purposes of argument, we consider a marginal investment for which the internal rate of return is no greater than the interest rate, the enterprise has a strong incentive to accelerate repayments as there is no real cost in so doing. The situation in which the rate of interest charged is equal to the internal rate of return is also illustrated in Tables 2.1 and 2.2 in the case of economic straight-line depreciation respectively under the general heading "Finance by loan". Net profits less interest charges on the amount of the loan outstanding are zero for every period when economic depreciation is used. The decline in net profits from period to period is exactly counterbalanced by the decline in interest payments. For straight-line depreciation, however, net profits less interest are initially negative but soon become positive and continue to increase throughout the project. Moreover, the positive and negative figures do not cancel each other out and there is a considerable positive balance over the project as a whole. It is this phenomenon which once again generates the illusion that the results obtained from the project as a whole are somehow more profitable when straight-line depreciation is used. Net profits minus interest payments are indeed greater on aggregate when straight-line depreciation is used, but only because additional funds are surreptitiously being ploughed back into the project without showing up in the balance sheet.

The valuation of assets

There is fairly general agreement among both economists and accountants that, in principle, depreciation should measure the decline in the value of a capital good during the accounting period in question. Thus, the consumption of fixed capital, the economist's term for depreciation, is defined as follows in the SNA[8].

The consumption of fixed capital is "the value, at current replacement cost, of the reproducible fixed assets... used up during a period of account as a result of normal wear and tear, foreseen obsolescence and the normal rate of accidental damage".

This definition may be compared with one recently proposed by a professional accounting body.

"Depreciation is a measure of the wearing out, consumption or other loss in value of a fixed asset which can arise from use, effluxion of time and obsolescence through technological and market changes. Assessment of depreciation and its allocation to accounting periods involves in the first instance consideration of three factors:

a) cost (or valuation when an asset has been revalued in the books);

b) the nature of the asset and the length of its expected useful life to the business having due regard to the incidence of obsolescence;

c) estimated residual value."[9]

The practical problem is to decide how a capital good is to be valued and how the change in this value is to be measured over time. The present section is concerned with situations in which the present value of the expected future profits from the use of a capital good exceeds its current cost or purchase price. This may happen even though the assumption of constant prices is retained, and the problems created by changing prices are examined in a later section.

The theory underlying economic depreciation tends to assume that the present value of the gross profits derived from the use of a capital good is equal to its purchase price. Such an assumption is made for convenience rather than of necessity, although it can be justified by arguing that in a competitive equilibrium forces of competition will eliminate any surplus of one over the other. In practice, however, it may be presumed that the present value of expected future gross profits discounted at the rate of interest on borrowed funds will usually exceed the cost of the capital good: otherwise the investment is scarcely likely to be undertaken. If the discount rate used to calculate the present value, which will be denoted by r^*, is less than the internal rate of return r, then

$$v_1^* = \sum_{i=1}^{n} f_i \,(1+r^*)^{-i} > k = v_1 \qquad (15)$$

where the use of the asterisk on the present value indicates that r^* has been used instead of r.

It is obvious that the decline in v^* from period to period does not provide an acceptable measure of depreciation. The expression $(v_i^* - v_{i+1}^*)$ measures the decline in the present value of the investment project from period to period as distinct from the decline in the value of the capital good employed. Such an expression sums to v_1^*, over the life of the project and v_1^* exceeds k by assumption as shown in (15). Depreciation, however, is a method of allocating the cost of using some capital good among different accounting periods and its total cannot exceed the cost of acquiring that good. The use of a capital good which is gradually consumed over the life of a project has to be treated as a

8. United Nations, *A System of National Accounts,* Glossary of main terms, p. 231.

9. Exposure Draft 15 of the ASSC, January 1975, *Accounting for depreciation* (London, 1975).

cost of production in the same way as the use of non-durable goods which are entirely consumed as intermediate inputs within a single accounting period. The length of the accounting period, or the frequency with which accounts are drawn up, cannot determine whether or not something is a cost of production. On the other hand, the total cost of using some good cannot exceed its current opportunity cost as reflected by its current price. It follows, therefore, that the sum of the depreciation provisions over the life of a project has to be identical with the cost of the capital good (less any residual or scrap value): assuming scrap values are zero, this implies

$$\sum_{i=1}^{n} d_i = k \tag{16}$$

which is taken to be an essential prequisite, or constraint, applying to any method of depreciation.

The measurement of depreciation and net profits is linked to the measurement of income in general. A widely accepted definition of income attributable to J.R. Hicks[10] is the following

$$y_i = f_i + v_{i+1} - v_i$$

$$\text{or } y_i = f_i - (v_i - v_{i+1}) \tag{17}$$

which coincides with net profits as defined here. Suppose, however, that the discount rate which is used is r*: in this case, a surplus is created at the time of the original investment because

$$\sum_{i=1}^{n} f_i \, (1+r^*)^{-i} - k = s > 0 \tag{18}$$

Substituting into (17) this surplus is treated as accruing entirely in period 0; thus if

$$y_o = f_o + v_1{}^* - v_o{}^*$$

then, given that

$$f_o = -k \text{ and } v_o{}^* = 0$$

$$y_o = v_1{}^* - k = s \tag{19}$$

None of the surplus is treated as income which accrues in the periods 1 to n when production actually takes place. Having allocated the entire surplus to period 0, the term $(v_i{}^* - v_{i+1}{}^*)$ has then to be used for purposes of calculating income or net profits in subsequent periods. This is an inflated "depreciation" provision which proceeds to write off as "depreciation" not merely k, the cost of the capital good, but also s, the surplus earned on it.

This is taking the accrual principle to absurd lengths. Given that the surplus is based on expected receipts from production which has not even started in period 0 when the surplus is recorded as accruing, it may be asked why the surplus should not be treated as accruing in the previous period when the entrepreneur conceived the idea that a profitable investment was possible and took the decision to proceed with it. While it is reasonable to argue that no income should be recorded until the capital expenditure is actually incurred, the same principle should also apply to the necessary current expenditures. Current and capital expenditure should be treated consistently: there is no justification for

10. There is a penetrating discussion of the concept of income in chapter XIV of J.R. Hicks' *Value and Capital* (Oxford, 2nd edition, 1946), pp. 171 to 188. It is worth noting, however, that Hicks begins his discussion (p. 171) by observing: "Nothing has been said about Income, about Saving, about Depreciation, or about Investment... In spite of their familiarity, I do not believe that they are suitable tools for any analysis which aims at logical precision. There is far too much equivocation about their meaning... At bottom, they are not logical categories at all; they are rough approximations, used by the business-man to steer himself through the bewildering changes of situation which confront him." Hicks eventually concludes (p. 180) that for the theoretical economist "income is a very dangerous term, and it can be avoided".

anticipating all current expenditure and no capital ones. And if everything can be anticipated an endless regression becomes possible with surpluses accruing at the same time as bright ideas are conceived.

The use of the internal rate of return as the discount rate avoids all these problems. In period 0 income must be zero because

$$v_1 = k, \ f_o = -k \ \text{and} \ v_o = 0$$

so that

$$y_o = f_o + v_1 - v_o = 0 \tag{20}$$

Although income, depreciation and net profits depend on expectations of future profits, income and net profits are recorded only as production takes place and gross profits are actually earned in periods 1 to n. Any surplus which is attributable to the rate of interest on borrowed funds being less than the internal rate of return will be gradually realised as a surplus of net profits over the related interest charges in a succession of subsequent accounting periods.

In this context, a distinction needs to be maintained between the cost of a capital good, from which depreciation charges are derived, and the present value of an investment project which uses that good as its only capital input. The two are not the same or else there would be no incentive to engage in the production process which uses the good. The decline in the value of the capital good to the enterprise has to be related to its planned use by that enterprise, which in turn links the depreciation charge to the associated sequence of expected gross profits, but only in conjunction with the constraint that the value of the good itself cannot exceed its cost so that depreciation charges must always sum to equal that cost, as expressed by (16). The decline in the value of the capital good which constitutes the depreciation charge must be calculated with reference to its use within that particular enterprise which implies using the internal rate of return as the discount factor to be applied to the sequences of expected gross profits. Otherwise, there is a variety of interest rates external to the enterprise which might be used to calculate present values and the choice of an interest rate becomes somewhat arbitrary. Even if the interest rate at which the enterprise itself is able to borrow were to be used, problems would arise whenever the rate changed. Depreciation charges do not change whenever interest rates change (although as explained in the previous section, the amounts which have to be transferred to a depreciation fund would be changed). On the other hand, a change in the sequence of gross profits would affect the calculation of depreciation. Suppose the sequence is shortened, perhaps because of unforeseen obsolescence: at that point, the internal rate of return should be recalculated leading to a lower figure for the project as a whole and hence a higher depreciation charge each period. The excess of the depreciation provisions which should have been accumulated up to that point over those actually accumulated is probably best treated as if a capital loss has been incurred which requires the remaining value of the capital good to be written down to that extent. Subsequent depreciation charges will still be higher than previously, however, even though the remaining value of the capital good is written down in this way. The substantive point is that depreciation charges are genuinely increased in the circumstances postulated, both for past and any future periods remaining, because reducing the lifetime of the capital good ipso facto increases the average cost per accounting period of using the capital good in this particular activity.

The cost of using some good, whether durable or not, in some productive process is given by its opportunity cost which may, in practice, be equated with its market price. It cannot cost the enterprise more than it can be bought for on the market. Moreover, it is this cost which must be used for purposes of calculating depreciation which is essentially a production cost. Any excess of the present value of a project using the good over the cost of the good may possibly be shown in the balance sheet under the heading of some item such as "goodwill", but any such excess is obviously not to be treated as if it constituted part of the value of the capital good itself. This line of reasoning is similar to that which advocates the use of the concept of "deprival" value as originally proposed by J.C. Bonbright[11] whereby the value of a good cannot exceed its current market price, however profitable its use may be in some particular activity. Even if the enterprise were to be deprived of the use of the good for some reason it can simply go out and buy another at the current market price. Of course, if the enterprise no longer found it profitable to replace it, its deprival value to the enterprise would be less than its price, but in no circumstance can it exceed the latter.

Depreciation with changing prices

It is convenient to distinguish changes in relative prices from changes in the general price level. The first case to be considered is one in which the price of the capital good changes relatively to other prices, and for simplicity it will be assumed that all other prices remain constant.

Changes in the relative price of the capital good

Suppose that the price of a particular capital good increases while all other prices remain constant. The immediate consequence is that the internal rate of return on a new project which uses that good is reduced and hence depreciation charges are increased for every period. The only question is whether the same applies to an existing project which is partially completed.

If the capital good which is partly used is non-transferable and quite specific to its existing use, it can be argued that an increase in the price of a new good of the same type is irrelevant and does not affect the cost of using the partly used good. To the extent that it is not specific, however, the cost of continuing to use the good in its present use must be increased when the opportunity exists for it to be used as a substitute for a new good for other purposes. Transferability need not imply change of ownership or physical movement: it merely implies the possibility of switching the capital good from the production of one good to another. There must be very few capital goods which are not transferable in this sense. For example, most buildings are transferable because many kinds of production can take place within them. There may be transfer or conversion costs, but these may be ignored in this context. A few structures such as bridges are quite specific, but they are rather exceptional. In any case, even a bridge is used by very many different economic units, and the relevant issue is the cost of using an existing asset for one purpose rather than another. Similarly, most types of machinery and equipment can be used in the production of various different goods or services. All transport equipment is transferable as are most standard machines such as lathes, drills, etc. There may be custom-built machinery which is quite specific, but again, it must be the exception rather than the rule.

So long as the opportunity exists of employing a partly used good as a substitute for a new one in the production of other goods, the cost of retaining it in its existing use must increase when the cost of the new good rises. In principle, the value of the partly used good should be revalued to equal what the value would be at the corresponding stage in the life of a new project just starting with the higher price capital good. This implies that the rate of return is lowered over

11. J.C. Bonbright, *The Valuation of Property* (McGraw-Hill, 1937), p. 71.

the remaining life of the project to the level applicable on a new project of the same type. As a result, depreciation charges are also increased over the remaining life. Net profits are correspondingly reduced in each subsequent period. This might even cause production to be ended and the asset to be transferred to some other use.

Although net profits are reduced in this way, the owner of a partly used capital good cannot be made worse off by an increase in the price of a new good. The owner receives a holding gain, or revaluation surplus, when the partly used capital good is revalued upwards and this counterbalances the reduction in the subsequent net profits or net operating surplus resulting from the higher depreciation charges. When owner and operator are the same economic unit, the reallocation from operating surplus to revaluation surplus could be regarded as a purely internal accounting transfer of no particular significance. From this point of view, it appears that the operator who is also owner is not substantially affected by an increase in the price of a new capital good when he is not engaged in any transactions in that good. However, while the total of the revaluation surplus plus the successive operating surpluses is the same as what the total of the operating surpluses would have been without the price increase in the capital good, the change is still significant. Revaluation and operating surpluses might be taxed differently, for example. In any case, the project ends with a higher accumulated depreciation fund than if the price increase had not occurred. The fund will not equal the cost of a new capital good, but it still may be substantially greater than if the price increase had not occurred. Obviously, the earlier in the life of the project the price increase occurs the closer the accumulated depreciation charges will approximate to the price of a new capital good, but they will always fall short. This can be a source of confusion if the increased depreciation charges are described as being justified on grounds of "replacement cost" accounting. The justification for the higher depreciation charges must rest on increased opportunity costs. The question of whether or not a capital good will be replaced is quite a separate issue, and the rationale underlying the increased depreciation is not the accumulation of a fund which is large enough to purchase a replacement at the new higher price. If the price increase occurs when the partly used good is nearing the end of its life, it is obvious that the increased depreciation charges will be quite inadequate to cover the increase in the cost of a new capital good. For these reasons, the use of the term "replacement cost" accounting will be avoided in this report so far as possible.

The owner/operator ends the project with a higher depreciation fund than would otherwise have been the case, the excess over the original cost of the capital good measuring the amount of the capital gain/holding gain/revaluation surplus (or whatever term is used). Although this is counterbalanced by an equal reduction in the total net operating surpluses earned, the change should exert some influence on the entrepreneur's behaviour, as the outcome of the project as a whole is patently different from what it would have been without the price increases. If the owner and operator are different economic units (as when capital goods are hired out to operators) the effects are by no means self cancelling, however, because the owner benefits from the revaluation surplus whereas the operator suffers the reduction in net profits. This is a simple example of the redistributional effects of changing prices.

Although the above argument has been conducted in terms of a single price increase coming part-way through the life of a project, it can easily be generalised to cover a succession of price increases or even a continuous price increase. Whenever the price of the capital good increases, or however often it increases, the depreciation charges associated with the use of that good should be correspondingly increased. The argument has, however, been conducted on the assumption that all other prices remain constant so that a price increase for an individual good does increase the real cost of using that good. It is now necessary to examine the other extreme in which there is general price inflation and all prices move up together.

Changes in the general price level

Suppose that all prices increase at a constant proportionate rate of 100 p per cent per period. An investment of k in period 0 will then generate the following sequence of monetary profits

$$f_1 (1+p),\ f_2 (1+p)^2,\ \ldots\ f_n (1+p)^n$$

where the f's denote the sequence of gross profits that would be earned if prices were to remain constant at their period 0 level. Working with discrete accounting periods it is convenient to assume that prices remain constant throughout each period and then jump instantaneously between the end of one period and the start of the next.

The internal rate of return can be defined in monetary or nominal terms as well as in real terms. The real rate of return at constant prices is defined in the usual way as the value of r which satisfies

$$\sum_{i=1}^{n} f_i (1+r)^{-i} = k \qquad (21)$$

The monetary or nominal rate of return m is defined as the value of m which satisfies

$$\sum_{i=1}^{n} f_i (1+p)^i (1+m)^{-i} = k \qquad (22)$$

It follows from (21) and (22) that the two rates of return are related as follows,

$$(1+m) = (1+r)(1+p) \qquad (23)$$

so that m exceeds r in the same way that monetary rates of interest exceed real rates.

Depreciation in period i may be defined as the change in the present value of the remaining sequence of f's between the beginning and end of period i measured at the prices of period i. This is, of course, the standard economic definition of depreciation, but is also makes explicit that when prices are changing from period to period the beginning and end of period values should both be measured at the prices of the period in question to ensure that they are commensurable with each other. Because prices are continually rising from one period to the next it is convenient to use present values expressed in terms of the monetary rate of return as follows:

$$v_i = (1+p)^i \sum_{x=i}^{n} f_x (1+p)^{x-i+1} (1+m)^{-(x-i+1)} \qquad (24)$$

$$= \frac{f_i (1+p)^{i+1} + v_{i+1}}{(1+m)} \qquad (25)$$

However, V_{i+1} is measured at the prices of (i+1) whereas V_i is measured at the prices of period i. It is necessary for purposes of measuring depreciation to measure V_{i+1} at the prices of i: in other words, to measure V_{i+1} at the end of period i as distinct from the start of period i+1. At this instant, the price increase between i and i+1 has not yet occurred, so that V_{i+1} at the prices of period i, which will be donated by $\widehat{V}_{i+1}$, is given by

$$\hat{v}_{i+1} = \frac{v_{i+1}}{1+p} \tag{26}$$

Equation (25) can now be rewritten as

$$v_i = \frac{f_i\,(1+p)^{i+1} + (1+p)\,\hat{v}_{i+1}}{(1+m)}$$

$$= \frac{f_i\,(1+p)^i + \hat{v}_{i+1}}{(1+r)} \tag{27}$$

so that depreciation is given by

$$d_i = v_i - \hat{v}_{i+1} = f_i\,(1+p)^i - rv_i \tag{28}$$

This is a straightforward generalisation of equation (5) to accommodate general price inflation. It is essential to note that each successive v_i is measured at its own prices and is therefore adjusted for inflation. The adjustment occurs when the present value of the remaining sequence of f's at the end of period i is revalued upwards at the start of period (i+1) by the factor (1+p). This adjustment is justified on the grounds that the prices of all the goods and services which determine the levels of the remaining sequence of f's measured in monetary terms are permanently increased by this factor betwen i and (i+1).

Net profits in period i are given by rv_i and it is obvious that the net accounting rate of return in period i (and indeed in every other period) is equal to the real internal rate of return when the present values of the assets are revalued in this way at the start of each period.

Although a revaluation surplus accrues at the start of each period, its implications are quite different from when such a surplus occurs because of a change in the relative price of the capital good employed. The surplus considered here is not at the expense of a reduced net operating surplus over the remainder of the project, nor does it reduce the internal rate of return. As the surplus accrues because of an increase in the monetary profits expected from the project it is clear that it should not have any adverse effect on subsequent net profits and rates of return. It is this kind of revaluation surplus which, in itself, is profitable to the owner of the asset, although as emphasised elsewhere in this report it is not legitimate to consider this surplus in isolation without reference to the decline in the purchasing power of the funds invested in the project. To the extent that these funds are borrowed from elsewhere, the owner of the asset receiving the revaluation surplus is the beneficiary in a net redistribution of wealth, but if he has invested his own funds the surplus is counterbalanced by an equal loss in the real purchasing power of those funds.

The analysis of the present section has been conducted on the assumption that all prices, including that of the capital good, rise by a uniform percentage. If the price of the capital good were to change by a different amount, its relative price would change which could be taken as an indication that its opportunity cost vis-à-vis other possible uses had also changed. It should be noted, therefore, that the revaluation surplus under consideration is not strictly attributable to the rise in the price of the capital good itself but to the general rise in prices including, in particular, those of the outputs from the process of production which uses that good. On the other hand, if the capital good were not to be revalued each period this would imply that its opportunity cost was steadily declining over time, which would be incorrect.

In practice, revaluations required either on the grounds of general inflation or a change in the relative price of the capital good can be accomplished simultaneously be a single adjustment based on the actual price change for a new capital good. If this increase is the same as that in the general price level, including the prices of the enterprise's own inputs and outputs, the receipt of the revaluation surplus does not affect subsequent profits and real rates of return. However, if an increase in the relative price of the good is super-imposed on a general price rise, the revaluation surplus is that much higher in the period in question, but only at the cost of lower operating surpluses and rates of return in the future. Conversely, of course, a relative price decline reduces the revaluation surplus but increases subsequent profitability.

Finally, if the capital good is deliberately not revalued, as happens with historic cost accounting, the revaluation surplus becomes entangled with, and indistinguishable from, the operating surplus. While this may not matter much in some circumstances if inflation is moderate, in general it would seem to be wholly undesirable. Revaluation and operating surpluses depend upon entirely different factors and the failure to distinguish one from the other seriously restricts the usefulness of the resulting profit figures. For example, there is the obvious risk that ballooning revaluation surpluses during a period of accelerating inflation may be mistaken for increased operating surpluses and real rates of return. Moreover, as shown in the following chapter, the failure to revalue assets can result in accounting rates of return which are so grossly inflated as to bear no resemblance whatsoever to underlying rates of return on investment.

Backlog depreciation

Suppose, for purposes of argument, that prices are stable except for a single increase in the price of the capital good which occurs half way through the life of the project. Assuming the asset is revalued at that time for reasons just given, then half of the depreciation provisions will refer to the old price and half to the new price. Their total will obviously fall short of the price of a new good, and the appropriation of additional sums to cover such a deficiency is known as "backlog" depreciation. Evidently, if prices are rising continually throughout the life of a project the total deficiency may be quite substantial if the provisions made for depreciation in the early periods relate to a price which was much lower than the final price. The size of the deficiency also depends on the depreciation method: the more accelerated the method is, the greater the deficiency will be.

If an enterprise operates a balanced set of projects retiring one capital good each period, no provision needs to be made for backlog depreciation provided current cost accounting is used. The total depreciation provisions on a balanced set of capital goods must equal the price of new machine, whatever depreciation method is used so long as it is applied consistently to all the goods. The depreciation provisions can be used to purchase a new capital good each period, and this situation can continue indefinitely, whatever the rate of inflation provided depreciation is always calculated at current costs.

The disappearence of backlog depreciation with a balanced set of projects is simply explained by the fact that all the depreciation provisions put aside each period are immediately spent on a new good. They are not allowed to depreciate in value over time and their instantaneous reinvestment in the capital goods used by the enterprise provides a perfect hedge against inflation. If, however, depreciation provisions are not reinvested in this way but in financial assets it may be difficult to obtain a rate of interest which is non-negative in real terms. This is the real problem with backlog depreciation when there is a firm intention to replace a capital good in the future.

In general, when current cost accounting is used the total accumulated depreciation provisions, while obviously falling short of the price of a new good, also greatly exceed the price of the old good being depreciated. Thus, whether the original good was financed by a bond or by a loan, a surplus gradually builds up as the price of a new good, which determines the depreciation charge, rises above the original purchase price which determined the size of the bond or loan. This surplus can be invested by the enterprise, and not merely the surplus itself but also the interest accumulated on it belong to the enterprise and remain at its disposal when it comes to the purchase of a replacement in the future. It may, perhaps, not be possible to invest the surplus at an interest rate which exceeds the rate of inflation, but that is quite another matter which has nothing to do with depreciation or its measurement. Moreover, if the original asset was indeed financed out of loan capital the enterprise gains considerably from inflation when it comes to the replacement. In these circumstances, the loan merely needs to be renewed at about the previous level in *money* terms because of the funds available from the additional depreciation charged plus the interest earned on that depreciation. Indeed, it is precisely by this kind of procedure that an enterprise is able to realise the whole of its revaluation surpluses, as explained in the following chapter. Alternatively, if the loan is renewed at a higher level equal to the current (replacement) cost of the capital good, the whole of the accumulated revaluation surpluses are then at the disposal of the enterprise for other purposes.

In conclusion, therefore, it should be noted, first, that "backlog depreciation" is not depreciation at all, in the sense that it has no connection with the cost of using a capital good within the accounting period in question. Second, it should not be represented as if it were an additional burden imposed by inflation. If depreciation provisions can be invested satisfactory either in new capital goods or in financial assets, the so-called problem disappears completely. If there is a problem it is an investment problem which has nothing to do with the production costs of the process of production which uses the capital good.

Depreciation for tax purposes

Depreciation is allowed as a cost of production for tax purposes. Other things being equal, enterprises have an incentive to claim as much depreciation as possible in the early periods, thereby deferring the payment of tax as long as possible. Other factors are relevant, of course, such as the possibility of future changes in taxes, but in general enterprises seem to prefer accelerating depreciation for tax purposes thereby increasing the present value of the stream of expected future profits after tax.

An OECD survey of tax depreciation practices[12], conducted in 1972, showed that the straight-line method was the one used predominantly for buildings in 16 Member countries and for equipment in 9 Member countries. The method is used to some extent or other in every country except one. The standard alternative to the straight-line method is the declining balance method which is a popular form of accelerated depreciation. A fixed percentage of the written down, or depreciated, value of the asset is charged as depreciation each period. Naturally, the percentage charged must exceed $\frac{100}{n}$ per cent, where n is the expected life of the asset, or the amount of depreciation charged will fall short of that under the straight-line method in every period after the first. A common procedure is the so-called double declining balance whereby

12. *International Comparison of Tax Depreciation Practices,* OECD (Paris, 1975), pp. 18, 19.

the percentage used is $\frac{200}{n}$. In France, for example, the rate of declining balance depreciation is computed by multiplying the rate of straight-line depreciation, i.e. $\frac{100}{n}$, by the following coefficients: 1.5 for assets with $n=3$ or 4; 2.0 for assets with $n=5$ or 6; and 2.5 for assets with $n > 6$. The countries in which the declining balance method is most popular appear to be Canada, Finland, Japan, Switzerland and the United States. Like straight-line depreciation, the declining balance method is used to some extent or other in almost every country.

The two basic methods of calculating depreciation just described, namely the straight-line and declining balance methods, are methods which are used both for internal accounting by businesses and also for the calculation of normal or ordinary depreciation allowances for tax purposes. The same firm may not necessarily use the same method for both purposes, but in some countries firms are required by law to use the same method, indeed the same figures, so that profit figures shown in the firm's own accounts, whether published or not, are identical with those on which it is taxed.

In most countries it has become customary to grant various special allowances in addition to the normal allowances based on one or other of the basic methods. The purpose of these special allowances is to influence the total amount of investment undertaken by firms or the pattern of investment between different industries or regions. The special allowances usually apply only to new investment. They reduce the level of taxable profits in quite arbitary ways depending on the objectives of government policy. As the levels of taxable profits may be manipulated in this way by government action they cannot be related to any underlying theoretical concept of profit. There seems little point in the present context, therefore, of doing more than describing the main kinds of special allowances which are used.

In general, the special allowances are intended to accelerate depreciation by enabling firms to bring forward their depreciation charges. A common method is to grant an initial allowance of x per cent in the first year where x greatly exceeds the percentage that would be chargeable under either of the standard methods. The balance of (100 — x) per cent is then depreciated by standard methods over the remaining life of the asset. Another method is simply to allow a firm to write off an asset in y years where y is less than the normal economic life of the asset, and sometimes considerably less. One or other of these methods of accelerating depreciation seems to have been used at some time or other by almost every OECD country. Certainly, the absence of any form of artificially accelerated depreciation is very much the exception than the rule. Of course, the extent of accelerated depreciation varies considerably among countries and it is usually used selectively to encourage particular types of investment. The limit seems to have been reached by the United Kingdom which has allowed 100 per cent depreciation on assets in the year in which the expenditure is incurred. If firms do not have high enough profits in the early periods they may wish to defer some of the accelerated depreciation to which they are entitled. Provision is usually made for this so that firms are not obliged to claim the special allowances in full if they do not wish to do so. For example, the 100 per cent allowances in the UK may be disclaimed, in which case the second method described above comes into play, firms being allowed to depreciate the assets at 25 per cent over four years.

It is possible to go beyond accelerated depreciation by granting special allowances which are additional to the normal allowances instead of replacing them. In this way, the total "depreciation" provisions may exceed 100 per cent of the cost of the original investment. Thus, a special allowance of x per cent may be granted in the first year while at the same time continuing the ordinary depreciation allowances. This type of allowance does not appear to have been used so extensively as accelerated depreciation, but it is still common. Once again it is typically granted selectively to stimulate particular kinds of investment, or investment in particular localities. To benefit from such an allowance, which is of course essentially a deduction from profits for purposes of taxation, the firm must have sufficiently large profits, as already noted. As this may not always be the case, the next step is to make a cash grant in respect of investment undertaken which the firms receive irrespective of its profits. At this point, however, it is possible to part company with the subject because investment grants of this kind are no longer deductions for purposes of assessing taxable profits, and they cannot conceivably be described as depreciation allowances.

This brief discussion of the various forms of accelerated depreciation practised and the various special forms of depreciation allowance which are granted, serves to underline the well known fact that the total of depreciation allowances granted for tax purposes cannot be used as measures of depreciation on either economic or business accounting definitions. The deliberate manipulation of tax allowances in the interests of general economic policy renders them useless for other purposes. Moreover, in most countries the extent of this manipulation is not trivial: massive changes in the scale of depreciation allowances have been made, as these have become a major instrument of economic policy making. It is necessary, of course, in the case of any individual country to check how extensively depreciation provisions have been manipulated, but there can be few countries in which depreciation allowances for tax purposes can be assumed to approximate closely to those required by orthodox accounting principles.

In conclusion, it may be noted that the case for accelerated depreciation has been argued in some countries on the grounds that ordinary depreciation provisions based on historic cost are quite inadequate in a period of rising prices. Accelerated depreciation has therefore been advocated, and apparently granted, to make good the deficiencies of historic cost accounting, thereby making the situation even more confused.

Alternative estimates of depreciation

Numerical estimates of depreciation are influenced by at least three sets of factors:

1. The valuation method used.
2. The depreciation formula adopted.
3. Arbitrary rules such as those imposed by legislation.

It is not possible to assess the relative importance of those factors in practice without a major research effort. Following a revision of the US national accounts a few years ago, an investigation of this kind was carried out and the results published[13]. A summary of the main results is given in Tables 2.4 and 2.5: the data in the original source cover the entire period from 1929 to 1975, but only the last decade is considered here.

Estimates of depreciation on alternative assumptions are made possible by utilising capital stock data compiled by the perpetual inventory method, data which themselves have only become available in the last few years. Given the capital stock figures, capital assumption can be estimated in different ways according to whether:

13. United States, *Survey of Current Business,* March 1976, pp. 53-56.

1. Historic or current replacement costs are used.
2. Straight-line or double declining balance depreciation methods are used.
3. Full service lives are assumed, or shortened lives.

The actual capital consumption allowances shown in the US national accounts are based on straight-line current replacement cost using 0.85 Bulletin F service lives. The significance of the latter point is that the original service lives for tax purposes are considered to be over-estimates and they have therefore been reduced by 15 per cent (they have also been reduced by varying amounts for tax purposes as a deliberate method of accelerating depreciation). In Table 2.4 the first column shows depreciation estimated by straight-line historic cost also using 0.85 service lives. A comparison between these figures and those given in the fourth column, which consist of the capital consumption estimates, shows the extent of the difference made by using historic cost accounting and replacement cost accounting, other things being equal.

In 1965 depreciation at historical cost was about 12 per cent lower than at replacement cost, but by 1975 it had fallen to 27 per cent below replacement cost. The fall was particularly sharp between 1973 and 1975. The gap between the two is not likely to narrow again quickly once it is established, even if inflation moderates. In Table 2.5 the resulting differences in net profits are examined. In 1965, net profits using historic costs exceeded those at replacement costs by about 6 per cent, but by 1975 this figures had climbed to 30 per cent. It should perhaps be made clear that the profit figures in both cases are after deducting stock appreciation.

The transition from historic cost straight-line depreciation to tax depreciation can be accomplished in two steps. First, the effects of switching from the straight-line to the double declining balance method are revealed by comparing columns (1) and (2) in Table 2.4. The use of double declining balance increases depreciation by about 12 or 13 per cent in each year without any noticeable time trend. The total depreciation provisions for a balanced stock of capital would be unaffected by the depreciation formula used, but accelerated depreciation will tend to increase total depreciation when investment has been growing. Moving from column (2) to (3) shows the impact of the various special allowances granted for tax purposes. In reality, the situation is more complicated because not all firms use the double declining balance formula, but it seems better on balance to compare columns (2) and (3) rather than (1) and (3). The relative importance of the various special allowances appears to have increased somewhat in recent years.

One of the more interesting features of the data is that they show that the combined effect of the various special allowances more than offset the effect of using historic costs until as recently as 1974. In other words, net profits as assessed for tax purposes were lower than they would have been using capital consumption based on replacement costs (without the special allowances, of course) until 1974. In 1974, however, the understatement of depreciation resulting from the use of historic costs during inflation eventually dominated the overstatement resulting from the various ad hoc special allowances, so that net profits for tax purposes finally exceeded those based on replacement cost depreciation.

Assuming that any change-over from historic cost accounting to replacement cost accounting is likely to be accompanied by a radical overhaul of the various special allowances, the data in the tables help to explain why there has not been very much pressure for a major reform of accounting procedures in the USA. Proposals for some form of current cost, or current purchasing power, accounting have been made periodically in the USA but without sense of urgency.

However, the situation revealed in the tables is a disturbing one, bearing in mind that inflation in the United States has not been so severe as in some other countries. It illustrates how much net profits can be inflated by revaluation surpluses when historic cost accounting is used. Moreover, the uneasy compromise which has been reached by extending in a somewhat piecemeal fashion various special depreciation allowances to counter-balance the effects of inflation is not a satisfactory solution. It may be surmised that a similar situation exists in most other countries even though corresponding data cannot be obtained, because special depreciation allowances are known to have proliferated in most countries, and often to a much greater extent than in the USA.

TABLE 2.1 ILLUSTRATIVE INVESTMENT PROJECT USING ECONOMIC DEPRECIATION

Period	Gross Profits	Economic depreciation	Net Profits (1)—(2)	Initial investment *less* accumulated depreciation	Rate of return (%) (3) / (4)	Finance by a bond		Finance by a loan	
						Interest earned on accumulated depreciation provisions	Net income =net profits plus interest earned (3)+(6)	Interest charge on loan outstanding	Net profits less interest charge (3)—(8)
	(1)	(2)	(3)	(4)	(5)	(6)	(7)	(8)	(9)
1	100	2.87	97.12	500.0	19.42	0	97.12	97.12	0
2	100	3.42	96.57	497.1	19.42	0.56	97.12	96.57	0
3	100	4.09	95.90	493.7	19.42	1.22	97.12	95.90	0
4	100	4.89	95.10	489.6	19.42	2.02	97.12	95.10	0
5	100	5.84	94.15	484.7	19.42	2.97	97.12	94.15	0
6	100	6.97	93.02	478.8	19.42	4.10	97.12	93.02	0
7	100	8.32	91.67	471.9	19.42	5.45	97.12	91.67	0
8	100	9.94	90.05	463.5	19.42	7.07	97.12	90.05	0
9	100	11.88	88.11	453.6	19.42	9.01	97.12	88.11	0
10	100	14.18	85.81	441.7	19.42	11.31	97.12	83.81	0
11	100	16.94	83.05	427.5	19.42	14.07	97.12	83.05	0
12	100	20.23	79.76	410.6	19.42	17.36	97.12	79.76	0
13	100	24.16	75.83	390.3	19.42	21.29	97.12	75.83	0
14	100	28.86	71.13	366.2	19.42	25.99	97.12	71.13	0
15	100	34.46	65.53	337.3	19.42	31.59	97.12	65.53	0
16	100	41.16	58.83	302.8	19.42	38.29	97.12	58.83	0
17	100	49.15	50.84	261.7	19.42	46.28	97.12	50.84	0
18	100	58.70	41.29	212.5	19.42	55.83	97.12	41.29	0
19	100	70.11	29.88	153.8	19.42	67.24	97.12	29.88	0
20	100	83.73	16.26	83.7	19.42	80.86	97.12	16.26	0
Total	2 000	500	1 500	7 724	19.42	442.40	1 942.40	1 500	0

TABLE 2.2 ILLUSTRATIVE INVESTMENT PROJECT USING STRAIGHT-LINE DEPRECIATION

Period	Gross Profits	Straightline depreciation	Net Profits (1)—(2)	Initial investment *less* accumulated depreciation	Rate of return (%) (3) / (4)	Finance by a bond: Interest earned on accumulated depreciation provisions	Finance by a bond: Net income =net profits plus interest earned (3)+(6)	Finance by a bond: Total investment[a]	Finance by a bond: Net investment	Finance by a loan: Interest charge on loan outstanding	Finance by a loan: Net profits less interest charge
	(1)	(2)	(3)	(4)	(5)	(6)	(7)	(8)	(9)	(10)	(11)
1	100	25	75	500	15.00	0	75	500	22.1	97.12	−22.12
2	100	25	75	475	15.78	4.86	79.86	522.1	21.6	92.25	−17.25
3	100	25	75	450	16.66	9.71	84.71	543.7	20.9	87.39	−12.39
4	100	25	75	425	17.64	14.57	89.57	564.6	20.1	82.54	−7.54
5	100	25	75	400	18.75	19.42	94.42	584.7	19.1	77.68	−2.68
6	100	25	75	375	20.00	24.28	99.28	603.8	18.1	72.83	2.17
7	100	25	75	350	21.42	29.13	104.13	621.9	16.6	67.97	7.03
8	100	25	75	325	23.07	33.99	108.99	638.5	15.1	63.11	11.89
9	100	25	75	300	25.00	38.84	113.84	653.6	13.1	58.26	16.74
10	100	25	75	275	27.27	43.70	118.70	666.7	10.8	53.41	21.59
11	100	25	75	250	30.00	48.55	123.55	677.5	8.0	48.55	26.45
12	100	25	75	225	33.33	53.41	128.41	685.5	4.8	43.70	31.30
13	100	25	75	200	37.50	58.26	133.26	690.3	0.9	38.84	36.16
14	100	25	75	175	42.85	63.12	138.12	691.2	−3.9	33.99	41.01
15	100	25	75	150	50.00	67.97	142.97	687.3	−9.5	29.13	45.87
16	100	25	75	125	60.00	72.83	147.83	677.8	−16.1	24.28	50.72
17	100	25	75	100	75.00	77.68	152.68	661.7	−24.2	19.42	55.58
18	100	25	75	75	100.00	82.54	157.54	637.5	−33.7	14.57	60.43
19	100	25	75	50	150.00	87.39	162.39	603.8	−45.1	9.71	65.29
20	100	25	75	25	300.00	92.25	167.25	558.7	−58.7	4.86	70.14
Total	2 000	500	1 500	5 250	28.57	922.50	2 422.50	12 474	0	1 019.61	480.39

a) Total investment = present value of remaining future gross profits plus accumulated depreciation provisions.

TABLE 2.3 INVESTMENT PROJECTS WITH FLUCTUATING AND DECLINING FLOWS OF GROSS PROFITS

Period	Gross Profits (1)	Economic depreciation (2)	Net Profits (1)—(2) (3)	Initial investment *less* accumulated depreciation (4)	Rate of return (%) (3) / (4) (5)	Gross Profits (6)	Economic =straightline depreciation (7)	Net Profits (6)—(8) (8)	Initial investment *less* accumulated depreciation (9)	Rate of return (%) (8) / (9) (10)
1	50	−44.88	94.8	500.0	18.97	167.86	25	142.86	500	28.57
2	100	−3.40	103.4	544.8	18.97	160.71	25	135.71	475	28.57
3	150	45.94	104.0	548.2	18.97	153.57	25	128.57	450	28.57
4	150	54.66	95.3	502.3	18.97	146.43	25	121.43	425	28.57
5	100	15.03	84.9	447.6	18.97	139.29	25	114.29	400	28.57
6	100	17.89	82.1	432.6	18.97	132.14	25	107.14	375	28.57
7	50	−28.71	78.7	414.7	18.97	125.00	25	100.00	350	28.57
8	50	−34.16	84.1	443.4	18.97	117.86	25	92.86	325	28.57
9	50	−40.64	90.6	477.6	18.97	110.71	25	85.71	300	28.57
10	100	1.64	98.3	518.2	18.97	103.57	25	78.57	275	28.57
11	100	1.95	98.0	516.6	18.97	96.43	25	71.43	250	28.57
12	150	52.32	97.6	514.6	18.97	89.29	25	64.29	225	28.57
13	200	112.15	87.7	462.3	18.97	82.14	25	57.14	200	28.57
14	150	83.55	66.4	350.1	18.97	75.00	25	50.00	175	28.57
15	50	−0.58	50.5	266.5	18.97	69.86	25	42.86	150	28.57
16	50	−0.70	50.7	267.1	18.97	60.71	25	35.71	125	28.57
17	150	99.16	50.8	267.8	18.97	53.57	25	28.57	100	28.57
18	25	−7.01	32.0	168.6	18.97	46.43	25	21.43	75	28.57
19	125	91.65	33.3	175.7	18.97	39.29	25	14.29	50	28.57
20	100	84.04	15.9	84.0	18.97	32.14	25	7.14	25	28.57
Total	2 000	500	1 500	7 902.7	18.97	2 000	500	1 500	5 250	28.57

TABLE 2.4 ALTERNATIVE ESTIMATES OF DEPRECIATION
UNITED STATES: NON-FINANCIAL CORPORATIONS
$ Billion

	Historic cost straight line (1)	Historic cost double-declining balance (2)	Actual tax allowances (3)	Replacement cost straight line (4)	(1) as % of (4) (5)	(2) as % of (4) (6)	(3) as % of (4) (7)
1965	29.0	32.0	36.4	32.8	88.4	97.6	111.0
1966	31.5	35.2	39.5	35.7	88.2	98.6	110.6
1967	34.2	38.6	42.9	39.8	85.9	97.0	107.8
1968	37.0	41.8	46.7	43.0	86.0	97.2	108.8
1969	40.1	45.3	51.3	47.8	84.0	94.8	107.3
1970	43.4	49.0	54.6	53.1	81.7	92.3	102.8
1971	46.7	52.3	58.7	58.2	80.2	89.9	100.9
1972	50.1	55.9	65.3	62.6	80.0	89.3	104.3
1973	54.4	61.0	70.3	68.7	79.2	88.8	102.3
1974	59.3	66.9	76.2	78.3	75.7	85.4	97.3
1975	64.8	73.1	84.0	89.0	72.8	82.1	94.3

Notes: Columns (1), (2) and (4) assume 85 F service lives (see original sources). Column (4) shows capital consumption as given in the National Accounts.

Source: Survey of Current Business: March 1976, pp. 53-56.

TABLE 2.5 EFFECTS ON NET PROFITS OF ALTERNATIVE METHODS
OF CALCULATING DEPRECIATION
UNITED STATES: NON-FINANCIAL CORPORATIONS
$ Billion

	Gross corporate profits (1)	Net profits based on depreciation calculated using: Historic cost straight line (2)	Historic cost double declining balance (3)	Actual tax allowances (4)	Replacement cost straight line (5)	(2) as % of (5) (6)	(3) as % of (5) (7)	(4) as % of (5) (8)
1965	99.0	70.0	67.0	62.5	66.1	105.9	101.4	94.6
1966	106.9	75.4	71.7	67.4	71.2	105.9	100.7	94.7
1967	106.5	72.3	67.9	63.6	67.2	107.6	101.0	94.6
1968	115.1	78.2	73.4	68.5	72.1	108.5	101.8	95.0
1969	114.2	74.1	68.9	62.9	66.4	111.6	103.8	94.7
1970	104.7	61.3	55.7	50.1	51.6	118.8	107.9	97.1
1971	116.9	70.2	64.7	58.2	58.7	119.6	110.2	99.1
1972	134.6	84.5	78.7	69.3	72.0	117.4	109.3	96.3
1973	144.6	90.2	83.6	74.3	75.9	118.8	110.1	97.9
1974	141.5	82.2	74.6	65.3	63.2	130.1	118.0	103.3
1975	168.2	102.9	94.6	84.2	79.2	129.9	119.4	106.3

Notes: All profit figures are after deducting stock appreciation. Columns (2), (3) and (5) assume .85 F service lives (see original source). Column (5) shows net profits as given in the national accounts.

Source: Survey of Current Business, March 1976, pp. 53-56.

Chapter 3

AVERAGE ACCOUNTING RATES OF RETURN

INTRODUCTION

The purpose of this chapter is to analyse the relationship between the average accounting rate of return observed over the life of an investment project and the internal rate of return on that project. It is not concerned with divergencies which may occur because the profit expectations on which the original internal rate of return was calculated may not be realised in practice: obviously, there may be all sorts of unforeseen happenings which may cause the internal rate of return which is eventually realised to turn out to be different from the one which was expected at the time the investment was originally made. This chapter is concerned with a simpler but more fundamental question: namely, supposing that the profit expectations are always realised, how do the rates of return which are calculated period by period from the data on profits and capital provided by accountants relate to the internal rate of return on the investment project? Are such rates of return, even when averaged over the entire life of the project, consistent with the internal rate of return on which the investment decision may have been based? An alternative to assuming that profit expectations are always realised is to view the whole analysis as being conducted ex post, as a kind of post mortem on a completed investment project. How does the average accounting rate of return calculated from the actual recorded profit figures over the project as a whole relate to the internal rate of return which was actually realised? Can we be sure, even after the event, that because the average accounting rate of return was greater for one project than another that its internal rate of return was also greater? In other words, how relevant is the kind of information provided by accountants, whether business or economic accountants, to the investment decisions taken by business men?

As already suggested in the previous chapters, yet another way of interpreting an average accounting rate of return is to construe it as being calculated for a balanced set of projects within a single accounting period[1]. This is undoubtedly the most useful way of interpreting an average rate of return in the present context as it is particularly relevant to macro-economic analysis in which profits and capital are aggregated across different projects or enterprises in a single period of time. A balanced set of projects implies a constant rate of gross investment. The analysis of this chapter is also extended to cover the situation in which the rate of gross investment is growing from period to period so that the age distribution of the projects in existence (i.e., the capital stock) is not uniform.

Some answers to the questions posed above have already been given in the previous chapter. One of the main points emerging from the previous chapter

1. In a balanced set of projects an equal number of projects is started and terminated each period so that the "ages" of the projects are evenly distributed.

was that the accounting rate of return, defined as net profits divided by the net capital stock, will only coincide with the internal rate of return if the depreciation charged each period is economic depreciation. The use of more accelerated forms of depreciation which include the method principally used in practice, namely straight-line depreciation, leads to accounting rates of return which are consistently higher than the internal rate. Of course, the real profitability of an investment project cannot be improved by manipulating the accounting methods by which the profits are recorded, and the explanation for the higher accounting rates of return observed when conventional depreciation methods are used is that the values of the capital stock figures used tend to be systematically under-estimated. The higher accounting rates of return are illusory or bogus if the written down values of the capital goods are incomplete as a statement of the capital employed. The depreciation which is conventionally charged in the early years of a project is usually greater than costs actually incurred in using the capital goods in question. It may be perfectly sound, prudent business practice to put aside into reserve in the early years larger amounts than would be needed in a risk free world in which profit expectations are always realised, but some of the so-called depreciation provisions should be treated as appropriations to a contingency reserve rather than as costs of production. By treating them literally as costs of production, they are deducted from the enterprise's capital and their omission leads to distorted rates of return which are biassed upwards in consequence. The argument has been spelled out in detail in the previous chapter and will not be repeated here.

The extent of the divergence between an average accounting rate of return and the corresponding internal rate of return obviously depends on the depreciation method used. Given a particular depreciation method, however, it also depends on various other parameters: in particular, on r the internal rate of return itself, n the number of periods over which a project continues, and g the rate of growth of the investment projects over which the average is calculated. If historic cost accounting is used, the divergence is also particularly sensitive to p, the rate of price inflation. The main objective of the present chapter is to explore the effects of the various parameters just listed on the divergence between the average accounting rate of return and the internal rate of return. It is proposed to identify those combinations of parameters which are likely to cause the two rates to deviate the most from each other: in other words, to establish the conditions under which the average accounting rate of return is likely to be most misleading when used as an indicator of the underlying internal rate of return. As might be expected, the most serious divergences are liable to occur when historic cost accounting is used during inflation, and quite absurd accounting rates of return may be recorded in these circumstances. Indeed, because historic cost rates of return may assume almost any level whatsoever during inflation, for a given underlying real internal rate of return, it is very doubtful whether they should be calculated and published when there is serious inflation because their significance is totally obscure and they are bound to mislead.

If, however, current cost accounting is used the gross distortions introduced by inflation can be eliminated. In that case, the relationship between the average accounting rate of return and the internal rate of return is confined to much narrower limits. It has been argued that, even when prices are constant, average rates of return are liable to be so divergent from internal rates as to make it impossible to draw any inferences about the latter from the former, but such claims appear to be greatly exaggerated. The various inter-relationships, and the effects of the various parameters, are examined in some detail in this chapter where it is shown that under a wide range of conditions one rate may provide a tolerable approximation to the other. It is true that there are circumstances in which the average accounting rate may greatly exceed the internal rate, for example when r and n are both large and when g is low or negative, but once such combinations of parameters are identified the user can recognise the circumstances in which the risks of observing greatly exaggerated accounting rates of return are greatest. By examining the various inter-relationships the user may also get an impression of the orders of magnitude involved so that it may be possible to achieve a very rough translation from one type of return to the other.

Upto this point, the average accounting rates of return under consideration have been net rates: that is, net profits divided by net capital. An alternative measure is the ratio of gross profits to gross capital. Such a measure is immediately attractive from a practical point of view because it by-passes completely all the problems involved in the proper measurement of depreciation, problems which take up so much of the contents of this report. In national accounting summary aggregates such as GDP or GNP have long since displaced the corresponding net measures, mainly for this very reason. Moreover, at a macro-economic level there is no doubt that gross measures of profits or capital are more readily available, more firmly based statistically and more easily interpreted. Although the whole problem of depreciation is by-passed, it is still not legitimate, of course, to use historic cost accounting, when compiling estimates of the gross capital stock: the cumulation of gross investment data measured at a succession of different prices is quite meaningless.

Given the practical advantages of rates of return based on gross measures, the important question becomes how useful such measures are analytically. In particular, how closely does a rate of return calculated as the ratio of gross profits to the gross capital approximate to the corresponding internal rate of return? While, as might be expected, the answer depends on a combination of parameters, one major conclusion emerging from the analysis of this chapter is that the average gross rate of return is likely to provide a closer approximation to the internal rate than the average net rate does over a very wide range of values of n and r. Moreover, the approximation may be very close indeed when n and/or r become large. Thus, it emerges that the average gross rate is likely to provide a close approximation in precisely those circumstances in which the average net rate is likely to be seriously biassed upwards, *and* vice versa. By calculating both rates, and choosing the lower or, possibly, an average of the two, the worst biasses which are liable to accur in accounting rates of return can be simply avoided. It is, therefore, recommended that both rates of return should be calculated whenever possible and this is the procedure adopted in chapter 6 of this report. It turns out that both rates are very similar at a macro level for countries with data available, a result which is not unexpected from the analysis of this chapter if r and n assume values in practice which are neither extremely small nor extremely large.

This chapter contains a great deal of theoretical analysis of accounting rates of return, some of which is fairly detailed. This introduction is intended to indicate the objectives behind the analysis and to point towards some of the main conclusions which eventually emerge.

Constant investments and constant prices

Consider a single investment project which generates a sequence of gross profits

$$f_1, f_2, \ldots f_i, \ldots f_n$$

over n periods. These gross profits denote the differences between current receipts and current operating costs each period before the deduction of depreciation. (They do not include any interest which is received or paid.) Unless specifically stated to the contrary, no restrictions are placed on the f's: they are not assumed to be constant or changing in any regular fashion, while individual f's may even be negative.

The value of the initial investment which generates this sequences of gross profits will be denoted by k. The investment is assumed to be made in period 0 before production takes place. The depreciation charged each period will be denoted by d_i and no general restrictions are placed on the d's except that they must sum to k over the life of the project so that the costs of the initial investment are fully charged against subsequent production. For convenience, scrap values are assumed to be zero so that

$$\sum_{i=1}^{n} d_i = k \qquad (1)$$

Three types of depreciation are considered. The first is economic depreciation which is defined in exactly the same way as in the previous chapter, namely,

$$d_i = v_i - v_{i+1} \qquad (2)$$

where

$$v_i = \sum_{x=i}^{n} f_x (1+r)^{-(x-i+1)} \qquad (3)$$

Thus, v_i denotes the present value at the beginning of period i of the remaining sequence of f's discounted at the internal rate of return r. It follows from equations (2) and (3) that

$$d_i = f_i - rv_i \qquad (4)$$

The properties of economic depreciation defined in this way were extensively discussed in the previous chapter and will not be repeated here.

The second type of depreciation is straight-line depreciation defined as

$$d_i = \frac{k}{n} \qquad (5)$$

which is obviously constant each period.

The third type of depreciation is the "sum-of-the-year's-digits" method as practised in the United States. This is used as an example of accelerated depreciation and is chosen because of its analytic convenience. It is defined as follows

$$d_i = \frac{n-i+1}{\sum_{i=1}^{n} i} k = \frac{2(n-i+1)}{n(n+1)} k \qquad (6)$$

Under this method, the depreciation charged each period declines at a linear rate from a figure of $\frac{2nk}{n(n+1)}$ in period 1 to $\frac{2k}{n(n+1)}$ in period n.

Net rates of return for individual periods

The accounting net rate of return, or ARR, is defined as gross profits minus depreciation divided by the value of the initial investment less the total depreciation provisions accumulated upto the beginning of the period: thus

$$ARR_i = \frac{f_i - d_i}{k - \sum_{x=1}^{i} d_{x-1}} \qquad (7)$$

where $d_0 = 0$.

When economic depreciation is used the denominator of this ratio is equal to v_i, as defined in (3) above, so that it follows from (4) that

$$\text{(economic depreciation) } ARR_i = \frac{f_i - d_i}{v_i} = r \tag{8}$$

Thus, the accounting rate of return coincides with the internal rate of return in every period, no matter what form the sequence of f's takes. This property was illustrated in the previous chapter.

It can also be proved that if the accounting rate of return is constant each period it must be equal to the internal rate of return. It follows, therefore, that the use of economic depreciation is both a necessary and a sufficient condition for obtaining an accounting rate of return which is equal to the internal rate of return in every single period throughout the life of the project.

When other methods of depreciation are used accounting rates of return for individual periods are not merely not constant but can be extremely variable. Thus, when straight-line depreciation is used, the ARR is given by

$$\text{(straight-line depreciation)} \quad {}_sARR_i = \frac{f_i - \frac{k}{n}}{k - (i-1)\frac{k}{n}} = \frac{nf_i - k}{k(n - i + 1)} \tag{9}$$

where the subscript s indicates straight-line depreciation. This expression tends to increase with i, although its behaviour also depends on the sequence of the f's. It is convenient to examine the special case where the f's are constant, in which case

$${}_sARR_i = \frac{nf - k}{k(n - i + 1)} = \frac{nG - 1}{n - i + 1} \tag{10}$$

where G is the gross accounting rate of return defined as

$$G = \frac{f_i}{k} = \frac{f}{k} \tag{11}$$

when the f's are all constant. It follows that the net return ${}_sARR$ increases from $G - \frac{1}{n}$ in period 1 to $nG - 1$ in period n: in other words, it increases by a factor of n. For example, when $n = 20$ and $G = 20$ per cent, the ${}_sARR$ increases from 15 per cent in period 1 to 300 per cent in period n. There is, therefore, a very strong built in tendency for the ${}_sARR$ to increase over the life of the project which will always manifest itself unless the f's decline sufficiently fast to counterbalance the progressive decline in the denominator of the ${}_sARR$.

The range of variation in the ${}_sARR$ is so great when the sequence of gross profits is fairly even that it is difficult to know what significance can be attached to it. The information conveyed by an ${}_sARR$ is likely to reflect the age of the project more than its inherent profitability. For example, a very high ${}_sARR$ probably indicates that a project is in its final stages and there can be no presumption that it reflects a high internal rate of return. Perhaps the only substantive point is to guard against the danger of making comparisons between the profitability of old and new projects which are heavily loaded against the latter. Were it not for the fact that the ${}_sARR$ becomes much more stable when it is averaged over a set of similar projects at varying stages of completion, it is doubtful whether the ${}_sARR$ could be treated as a meaningful or useful statistic.

The situation is even worse when an accelerated method of depreciation is used. Thus, using the sum-of-the-years-digits method

(accelerated depreciation)

$$ {}_{a}ARR_i = \frac{f_i - \dfrac{2(n-i+1)k}{n(n+1)}}{k - \sum_{x=1}^{i-1} \dfrac{2(n-x+1)k}{n(n+1)}} \qquad (12) $$

where the subscript a indicates accelerated depreciation. With constant f's this becomes

$$ {}_{a}ARR_i = \frac{(n+1)(nG-2)+2i}{(n+1)(n+2)-i(2n+3-i)} \qquad (13) $$

This expression can, to all intents and purposes, assume almost any value whatsoever over the life of the project. For example, when $n=20$ and $G=20$ per cent, the value of this expression increases from 10.5 per cent in period 1 to 4,100 per cent in period n. All the worst features of the net accounting rate of return based on straight-line depreciation are greatly magnified when accelerated depreciation is used. It is even possible for expression (13) to be negative in the early periods if $nG < 2$.

There is little point in spending further time on net accounting rates of return for individual periods based on straight-line or accelerated depreciation when they are so variable over the life of the project. They tend to start out well below the internal rate of return in the early stages of a project and finish up at vastly higher levels. At some point, therefore, they must be approximately equal to the internal rate of return. Experiments with simulated data suggest that when straight-line depreciation is used the two rates are equal about 40 per cent of the way through the life of the project. The longer the life of the project, the earlier the point at which the two rates are likely to be equal to each other.

Average net accounting rates of return

Rates of return may be averaged by aggregating the net profits earned in different periods and dividing by the aggregate of the net capital stocks existing in each period. In effect, the average is computed as the ratio of average profits to average capital. It can also be construed as a weighted average of the rates of return for individual periods in which the rates are weighted according to the sizes of the written down capital outstanding at the beginning of each period. As already stated, it is equivalent to the rate of return which would be observed for a balanced set of projects owned by a single enterprise or group of enterprises.

Using k_i to denote the value of the initial investment less the accumulated depreciation charged upto the beginning of period i, the average net accounting rate of return, AARR, is defined as

$$ AARR = \frac{\sum_{i=1}^{n} (f_i - d_i)}{\sum_{i=1}^{n} k_i} \qquad (14) $$

When economic depreciation is used $k_i = v_i$, and the AARR is obviously equal to r, given that the ARR is equal to r in every single period.

In general, it can be shown that

$$ \sum_i k_i = \sum_i i d_i \qquad (15) $$

so that (14) may be written as

$$\text{AARR} = \frac{\sum_i f_i - k}{\sum_i id_i} \tag{16}$$

One important property of the AARR is that it is independent of the distribution of the f's among different accounting periods. So long as they use the same depreciation methods, two projects with the same total gross profits and same initial investment must have the same AARR even though the gross profits may be distributed quite differently over time.

When straight-line depreciation is used, the value of the AARR depends on only two parameters F and n, where F is defined as the ratio of total gross profits to the level of the initial investment. With straight-line depreciation

$$\sum_i id_i = \frac{k}{2}(n+1) \tag{17}$$

and the AARR becomes

$$_s\text{AARR} = \frac{2(F-1)}{n+1} \qquad \text{where } F = \frac{\sum f_i}{k} \tag{18}$$

With the further assumption that the f's are all constant $F = nG$ so that

$$_s\text{AARR} = \frac{2(nG-1)}{n+1} \tag{19}$$

Thus, when $n = 1$ the $_s\text{AARR} = G - 1$ while for large values of n the $_s$AARR is approximately equal to 2G. For a given value of G, therefore, the net average accounting rate of return is an increasing function of n tending to an upper limit of 2G as n tends to infinity. The relationship between the gross and net accounting rates of return is considered further in the next section.

An expression can also be derived for the average accounting rate of return for accelerated depreciation when the sum of the years' digits method is used. It can be shown that

$$_a\text{AARR} = \frac{3(F-1)}{n+2} \tag{20}$$

whatever the sequence of the f's. This expression is very much simpler than the corresponding expression for a single accounting period, namely (13) above, and it also depends only on the two parameters, F and n. With the additional assumption of constant f's it can be seen that this expression increases from $G - 1$ when $n = 1$ to an upper limit of 3G as n tends to infinity.

It is necessary to examine how expressions (18) and (20) for the average net accounting rates of return when straight-line and accelerated depreciation are used are related to the internal rate of return. First, it may be noted that the AARR based on accelerated depreciation is always greater than that based on straight-line depreciation: the ratio of (20) to (18), namely,

$$\frac{_a\text{AARR}}{_s\text{AARR}} = \frac{3(n+1)}{2(n+2)} \tag{21}$$

is greater than unity (provided $n > 1$) and tends to an upper limit of 1.5 as n tends to infinity. Although this ratio is independent of F it is tacitly assumed, of course, that any two projects being compared do have the same values for F and n.

When $n = 1$ both expressions (18) and (20) are equal to $G - 1$, as already noted. Now,

$$G - 1 = \frac{f - k}{k} = r \qquad (22)$$

by definition of r when there is only a single period. Thus, all three AARR's based on economic, straight-line and accelerated depreciation initially assume the same value when there is only a single accounting period (or the accounts are consolidated for the project as a whole). If the additional assumption is made that the f's are all constant the three upper limits are known as the number of accounting periods is increased: namely,

economic depreciation: AARR $\rightarrow$ G as $n \rightarrow \infty$
straight-line depreciation: AARR $\rightarrow$ 2G as $n \rightarrow \infty$
accelerated depreciation: AARR $\rightarrow$ 3G as $n \rightarrow \infty$

The ranking of the three measures is the same as in the limit whenever n is greater than unity, although the AARR based on straight-line depreciation is usually considerably less than twice the internal rate of return over the range of values of n which are relevant to investment projects. If the assumption of constant f's is retained it is possible to obtain analytically an expression for the ratio of the AARR based on straight-line depreciation to the internal rate of return. With constant f's the internal rate of return is given by

$$f \sum_{1} (1+r)^{-i} = k \qquad (23)$$

and the series to be summed is a geometric progression. Hence,

$$f \left\{ \frac{(1+r)^n - 1}{r(1+r)^n} \right\} = k \qquad (24)$$

which on re-arrangement gives

$$r = G \left\{ \frac{(1+r)^n - 1}{(1+r)^n} \right\}$$

$$\text{or } r = G\,[1 - (1+r)^{-n}] \qquad (25)$$

This expression shows explicitly how $r \rightarrow G$ as $n \rightarrow \infty$. From (19) and (25) it follows that

$$\frac{{}_s\text{AARR}}{r} = \frac{2\,[(nr - 1)(1+r)^n + 1]}{r(n+1)\,[(1+r)^n - 1]} \qquad (26)$$

Numerical values of this ratio are given in Table 3.1 for various combinations of r and n. It can be seen that the ratio gradually increases from 1 to 2 as n increases, but it remains well below 2 over the range of values illustrated in the table.

TABLE 3.1 RATIO OF AARR TO THE INTERNAL RATE OF RETURN
(*Assuming constant profits per period and linear depreciation*)

Internal rate of return *r*	Number of periods: *n*					
	5	10	15	20	25	30
.05	1.033	1.073	1.113	1.152	1.191	1.228
.10	1.063	1.141	1.215	1.285	1.349	1.408
.15	1.092	1.203	1.304	1.394	1.471	1.535
.20	1.120	1.259	1.380	1.480	1.559	1.621
.25	1.146	1.310	1.443	1.546	1.623	1.680
.30	1.170	1.354	1.496	1.597	1.669	1.721

The ratios illustrated assume constant gross profits per period. If the same total gross profits over the project as a whole are redistributed so that they decline from period to period, it can be inferred that the internal rate of return r must be increased whereas the average accounting rate of return based on straight-line depreciation is unchanged because it is independent of the sequence of gross profits as already indicated. Thus, without further calculation, it can be inferred that a similar set of ratios based on a declining sequence of f's will all tend to be smaller than those illustrated in Table 3.1 (and vice versa, of course, if the f's are increasing). For these reasons, an average net accounting rate of return using straight-line depreciation may provide a fairly close approximation to the internal rate of return when the sequence of f's is declining, especially if neither r nor n are very large. The decline in the f's would have to be very substantial, however, to raise the internal rate of return above the accounting rate; the situation in which both rates are equal is illustrated in Table 2.3 of the previous chapter.

It has already been emphasised that total net profits over the life of a project are the same whatever the method of depreciation used. It follows, therefore, that ratios such as those illustrated in Table 3.1 are actually measuring no more than the ratios of the average capital stock figures which enter into the denominators of the rates of return. Thus, the ratios in Table 3.1 can be given a second and quite different interpretation because they also measure the ratio of the average capital stock figures based on economic depreciation and straight-line depreciation respectively. They can be interpreted, therefore, as measures of the extent to which the capital invested in projects is under-estimated on average as a result of the use of straight-line depreciation. When accelerated depreciation is used the under-estimation is aggravated: thus, all the ratios in Table 3.1 need to be multiplied by the factor $\frac{3(n+1)}{2(n+2)}$ to convert them into the corresponding ratios obtained when the sum of the years' digits method of depreciation is used.

Gross rates of return

The gross accounting rate of return has already made its appearance in the previous section. It is defined simply as the ratio of gross profits to the value of the initial investment. Denoting the gross rate of return in period i by G_i

$$G_i = \frac{f_i}{k} \tag{27}$$

It has the great attraction that it does not require any estimate of depreciation to be made in any period. It has the same kind of practical appeal which GDP or GNP has long exercised over Net National Income for economists. Indeed, its appeal is even greater because depreciation enters in a crucial way into both the numerator and the denominator of a net accounting rate of return. It is, therefore, important to establish how it is related to the net accounting rate of return and, in particular, to the internal rate of return.

In the "one-hoss shay" case, the gross rate of return (in marked contrast to the net rate) is obviously constant from period to period and equal to $\frac{f}{k}$. When the subscript i is dropped from G_i it should be understood that G refers to this constant rate $\frac{f}{k}$. Averaging the gross rate over the project as a whole, or over a balanced set of projets, presents no problems as the denominator of the gross return is always constant. Thus,

$$\overline{G} = \frac{\sum_i f_i}{nk} = \frac{\overline{f_i}}{k} \tag{28}$$

Assuming that the f's are all constant, the relationships between G and the three average net accounting rates of return may be obtained by re-arranging expressions (19), (20) and (25) above. Thus,

economic depreciation:

$$G = \frac{r\,(1+r)^n}{(1+r)^n - 1} = \frac{r}{1-(1+r)^{-n}} \tag{29}$$

straight-line depreciation:

$$G = \frac{{}_sAARR\,(n+1)}{2n} + \frac{1}{n} \tag{30}$$

accelerated depreciation:

$$G = \frac{{}_aAARR\,(n+2)}{3n} + \frac{1}{n} \tag{31}$$

When $n=1$, $G=1+r$ while as $n \to \infty$ $G \to r$, as already noted. The greater the number of periods over which a constant stream of f's are received, the closer the situation resembles that of a bond which generates an income stream in perpetuity. Looked at from this point of view, it is easy to see why $G \to r$ as $n \to \infty$. Moreover, G approaches r fairly quickly whenever r itself is not very small. This is illustrated in Table 3.2 in which the ratio of G to r is displayed for various combinations of r and n: for example, whenever $n > 15$, G exceeds r by much less than 10 per cent when $r > 0.2$.

It can be seen from (30) that as $n \to \infty$ $G \to \frac{1}{2}\,{}_sAARR$. The reason for this is simply that with straight-line depreciation the size of the net capital stock is approximately half that of the gross stock, *on average,* no matter how many periods are involved. As n becomes large the deduction from gross profits for depreciation becomes relatively less and less important, but the net capital stock is still only a half the gross stock on average so that in the limit the net ${}_sAARR$ tends towards a figure which is twice G and hence also twice r. A similar process of reasoning can be used to explain why $G \to \frac{1}{3}\,{}_aAARR$ when accelerated depreciation is used.

TABLE 3.2 RATIO OF GROSS RATE OF RETURN G TO INTERNAL RATE OF RETURN *r*

(*Assuming constant f's*)

Internal rate of return *r*	Number of periods: *n* 5	10	15	20	25	30
.05	4.619	2.591	1.927	1.605	1.419	1.301
.10	2.638	1.627	1.315	1.175	1.102	1.061
.15	1.989	1.328	1.140	1.065	1.031	1.015
.20	1.672	1.193	1.069	1.027	1.011	1.004
.25	1.487	1.120	1.036	1.012	1.004	1.001
.30	1.369	1.078	1.020	1.005	1.001	1.000

In general, $G > AARR$ for low values of n whether straight-line or accelerated depreciation is used: on the other hand, $AARR > G$ for high values of n. Except in the trivial case in the which $n = 1$, however, both G and the AARR are always greater than r, the internal rate of return. It follows, therefore, that the net AARR provides a closer approximation to r when n is low, but there must come a switch point as n increases at which G provides the closer approximation. Strictly, this conclusion has been deduced on the assumption of constant f's, and some qualifications to it are given later.

Assuming constant f's, the switch points occur when

$$G = {}_sAARR = \frac{2\,(nG - 1)}{n + 1} \qquad (32)$$

or when $G = \frac{2}{n - 1}$. It is more interesting to compute the switch points in relation to r rather than G, in which case the equation defining the switch points is given by

$$G = \frac{2}{n - 1} = \frac{r}{1 - (1 + r)^{-n}}$$

$$\text{or, } r = \frac{2\,[1 - (1 + r)^{-n}]}{n - 1} \qquad (33)$$

Some combinations of r and n which satisfy (33) are given in Table 3.3.

TABLE 3.3

Switch points[a]			
r	*n*	*r*	*n*
.839	3	.085	20
.410	5	.067	25
.271	7	.055	30
.180	10	.050	33
.134	13	.040	41
.115	15	.033	50
.100	17	.016	100

a) Combinations of *r* and *n* for which average gross and net accounting rates of return are equal (assuming constant *f*'s).

In practice, all the switch points lie very close to a rectangular hyperbola which can be represented by the equation

$$r\,(n - 1) = 1.6 \qquad (34)$$

the approximation being closest for large values of n. The equation derives from the fact that $(1 + r)^{-n} \approx 0.2$ for all combinations of r and n which satisfy (33). It follows from equations (33) and (34) that $\frac{G}{r}$ is approximately constant and equal to $\frac{5}{4}$, or 1.25, at all switch points: obviously, by definition of the switch points, the ratio of the average net accounting rate of return to r is also approximately equal to 1.25 along the curve described by equations (33) and (34).

If the decision rule is adopted of choosing whichever is the lower of the gross or net average accounting rates of return, the ratio of the resulting figure to the internal rate of return can never exceed 1.25 when the f's are constant. Equations (33) and (34) describe a ridge such that, for a given value of r, the ratio $\frac{\text{AARR}}{r}$ must be less than 1.25 for all values of n below the switch point, whereas the ratio $\frac{G}{r}$ must be less than 1.25 for all values of n above the switch point: each of the two ratios declines towards unity the further away n is from the ridge described by the switch points.

Grossly inflated average accounting rates of return are liable to be recorded in practice by using net rates in regions where gross rates are appropriate (i.e. when r and n are large) or by using gross rates in regions where net rates are appropriate (i.e. when r and n are small). By choosing the lower of the two, grossly misleading results can be avoided. Moreover, if r and n assume intermediate values and happen to lie in the vicinity of the curve describing the switch points, it is perfectly possible for both the gross and the net average accounting rates of return to yield very similar results.

If, instead of assuming constant profits, the possibility of declining profits is allowed for these conclusions have to be modified somewhat. When most profits are received in the early stages of an investment project, the internal rate of return r is considerably enhanced whereas the average gross and net accounting rates depend only on the total profits received and not on their distribution over time. For these reasons, it is possible for r to be greater than $\overline{G}$ when profits decline and also r and n are large. Thus, ${}_s\text{AARR}$ and $\overline{G}$ may lie on either side of r in these circumstances, which suggests that a simple average of the two accounting rates may provide the best indicator of r. Indeed, it is even theoretically possible for both accounting rates to lie below r if profits fall off so sharply that their rate of decline is faster than that implied by equation (8) of Chapter 2 above. While such cases might conceivably occur occasionally, it is difficult to believe that, *in general,* profits tend to decline nearly so fast as this so that taking an average of the two rates would appear to be the best strategy when the typical trend in profits is believed to be downwards. In any case, however, there is no justification for ignoring the valuable information provided by the average gross rate when it seems likely to approximate to the internal rate as least as closely as the average net rate does over a wide range of possible cases.

Growth with constant prices

Net accounting rates of return for individual periods tend to increase considerably over the life of a project when straight-line depreciation is used unless gross profits tend to decline rapidly from period to period. If the rate of investment has been growing over time the set of projects in existence in any one period cannot be evenly balanced because a greater proportion will still be in their early stages. This will tend to reduce the average or aggregate net accounting rate of return, so that net AARR's are influenced by the rate of growth, and in this section the effects of growth on net AARR's will be investigated.

Before so doing, it may be noted that the average gross rate of return is not nearly so sensitive to the rate of growth. If the sequence of f's associated with an individual investment project is constant, the average gross rate of return is invariant to growth. whereas the net rate is strongly influenced by growth in these circumstances. This greatly simplifies the interpretation and analysis of average gross rates of return although when the sequence of f's tends systematically to decline (or increase) over the life of a project, even average gross rates of return become influenced by growth. Only net accounting rates which utilise economic depreciation are independent of growth because they are constant from one period to another whatever the sequence of f's.

Consider, as before, a standard project which yields the following sequence of gross profits,

$$f_1, f_2, \ldots f_i, \ldots f_n$$

which need not conform to any regular pattern, from an investment equal to k in value. Let it be assumed that the size of this investment, and of the accompanying sequence of gross profit figures, can be scaled up or down by multiplying them by any number. Let it be further assumed that a firm has been investing a growing amount in such a project over at least the previous n periods and that it is proposed to calculate the firm's accounting rate of return, which is equivalent to the net AARR over the n projects initiated in the preceding n periods. Finally, let it be assumed that the level of investment in the current period is equal to k so that previous levels of investment were less than k, assuming growth was positive. This effectively fixes the current period as the base period for analytical purposes.

If the firm has been investing in this project an amount which grows by 100 g per cent each period, the profits received from the investment made in the previous period are equal to

$$\frac{f_1}{1+g}$$

and, in general, the profits received from an investment made i periods ago are equal to

$$\frac{f_i}{(1+g)^i}$$

Thus, total profits received in the current period are given by

$$F=\sum_{i=1}^{n}\frac{f_i}{(1+g)^i} \tag{35}$$

Similarly, it follows that total depreciation charges in the current period are equal to

$$D=\sum_{i=1}^{n}\frac{d_i}{(1+g)^i} \tag{36}$$

The total book value of all surviving assets in the current period is given by

$$K=\sum_{i=1}^{i=n}k\,(1+g)^{-i}-\sum_{i=1}^{i=n}\left\{(1+g)^{-i}\sum_{x=i}^{x=i}d_{x-1}\right\} \tag{37}$$

By rearranging the terms in the last expression in (37) in can be shown that

$$\sum_{i=1}^{i=n}\left\{(1+g)^{-i}\sum_{x=1}^{x=i}d_{x-1}\right\}=\frac{1}{g}\sum_{i=1}^{n}d_i\,(1+g)^{-i}-\frac{1}{g}\,\frac{\sum_{i=1}^{n}d_i}{(1+g)^n} \tag{37.1}$$

Equation (37) can then be written

$$K=k\,\frac{(1+g)^n-1}{g\,(1+g)^n}+\frac{1}{g}\,\frac{k}{(1+g)^n}-\frac{1}{g}\sum_{i=1}^{n}d_i\,(1+g)^{-i} \tag{37.2}$$

which can be further reduced to

$$K = \frac{1}{g} \left\{ k - \sum_{i=1}^{n} d_i (1+g)^{-i} \right\} \tag{38}$$

$$\text{or } K = \frac{k - D}{g} \tag{39}$$

assuming $g \neq 0$. On re-arrangement, this gives

$$\frac{k - D}{K} = g \tag{40}$$

As the book value of all surviving assets K is a measure of the net capital stock, equation (40) shows that net investment divided by the net capital stock, i.e. the measured rate of growth of the net capital stock, is always equal to g, whatever the depreciation method used, so long as it is applied consistently to all assets.

The accounting rate of return for this firm—that is, the AARR recorded for a series of standard investment projects growing at the rate g per period—is given by

$$AARR = \frac{F - D}{K} = g \frac{(F - D)}{k - D} \tag{41}$$

where F and D are defined above in (35) and (36) and K is given by (39). A special case of considerable theoretical interest is when $k = F$, or when the gross investment undertaken each period is equal to the gross profits received that period. It follows from the definition of the internal rate of return r that

$$\text{if } k = F \text{ then } g = r$$

$$\text{given that } F = \sum f_i (1+g)^{-i}$$

However, it also follows from equation (41) that if $k = F$, then $AARR = g$. Thus, in general, when $k = F$,

$$AARR = g = r \tag{42}$$

The converse also holds, namely when $g = r$ it follows that $k = F$

$$\text{so that } AARR = r$$

Thus, if the rate of growth of investment is equal to the internal rate of return, then the average net accounting rate of return is always equal to the internal rate of return, no matter what depreciation method is used. In deriving equations (41) and (42) no assumptions were made about either the sequence of f's or the sequence of d's, other than that

$$\sum_{i=1}^{n} d_i = k$$

The results obtained are independent of the depreciation formula used, provided only that the same formula is always used and that the cost of each investment made is recovered in full in subsequent depreciation charges. In effect, the depreciation method becomes irrelevant under the conditions assumed. Some insights into the reasons for this may be gained by remembering that the purpose of depreciation it to enable net profits to be calculated, net profits being the amounts which may be withdrawn from the business each period and disposed of in other ways. If, however, as a matter of policy gross investment always absorbs the whole of gross profits, nothing is ever withdrawn from the business and the calculation of depreciation and net profits become superfluous[2].

2. The analogous situation in the absence of growth would be a balanced set of projects with zero internal rate of return so that $k = \Sigma f_i$: in such a hypothetical situation, net profits and the AARR would always be zero whatever the depreciation method used, given also that $\Sigma d_i = k$.

These results are closely related to a number of basic propositions in the theory of economic growth. If a firm which is entirely self financing systematically ploughs back the whole of its profits each period into new investment, its profitability imposes an upper limit to its rate of growth. The internal rate of return is the maximum rate at which such a firm can grow. If gross profits are always immediately re-invested the firm becomes a closed system in which this maximum growth rate is achieved and can be sustained indefinitely. The analogy with equilibrium growth models such as Von Neumann's is clear. A firm behaving in this way can dispense with its accountants: whatever procedures are used, the accounting rate of return will equal the internal rate of return whenever the rate of growth is maximised in this way. With access to outside finance, of course, there is no upper limit to the rate of growth, so that values of g which are greater than r may perfectly well occur in practice.

As both current profits F and current depreciation charges D are functions of the growth rate g, it is not possible to infer from equation (41) how the AARR varies with g. In particular, it would be quite wrong to conclude from the way equation (41) is expressed that the AARR is an increasing function of g. In order to see how the AARR varies with g it is necessary to specify the forms taken by the sequences of f's and it is convenient to take up again the "one hoss shay" example in which the f's are constant. If, in addition, straight-line depreciation is assumed the series of profits and depreciation charges denoted by F and D in equation (41) become geometric progressions which yield, after some re-arrangement, the following expression

$$_{s}AARR = (nG - 1)\frac{g\,[(1+g)^n - 1]}{(ng - 1)\,(1+g)^n + 1} \qquad (43)$$

$$= (nG - 1)\,\Phi \qquad (44)$$

where Φ denotes the complicated expression involving g and n in equation (43). It can be shown that Φ is a decreasing function of g. Strictly, Φ is not defined when $g = 0$ but $\Phi \rightarrow \frac{2}{n+1}$ as $g \rightarrow 0$, and in fact the value of $_{s}AARR$ when $g = 0$ has already been given in equation (19) above. With increasingly rapid growth $\Phi \rightarrow \frac{1}{n}$ as $g \rightarrow \infty$ while with increasingly rapid negative growth $\Phi \rightarrow 1$ as $g \rightarrow -1$. Thus, the limiting values of (43) or (44) are as follows

$$_{s}AARR \rightarrow (nG - 1) \quad \text{as } g \rightarrow -1$$

$$_{s}AARR \rightarrow \frac{2\,(nG - 1)}{n+1} \quad \text{as } g \rightarrow 0$$

$$_{s}AARR \rightarrow G - \frac{1}{n} \quad \text{as } g \rightarrow \infty$$

Thus, when n is very large, the value of the $_{s}AARR$ falls from approximately 2G down to a lower limit of G as growth becomes increasingly rapid. With a large n G is also approximately equal to r. When n is small, however, the situation is more complicated and the $_{s}AARR$ falls significantly below G to a lower limit of $G - \frac{1}{n}$. This lower limit is the net accounting rate of return in period 1 of the standard investment project, namely

$$\frac{f - \frac{k}{n}}{k} = G - \frac{1}{n} \qquad (45)$$

and the *average* net accounting rate of return tends to this figure as $g \to \infty$. For example, it can be seen in Table 2.2 that in period 1 the net rate of return is only 15 per cent, whereas G=20 per cent and r=19.4 per cent. This also illustrates that as the $_s$AARR falls below G towards this lower limit, somewhere in the process it will coincide with r, at which point g=r.

It is not proposed to give any further numerical illustrations of the effects of g on the $_s$AARR at this point, because some illustrative data are given in the following section when the effects of changing prices are also allowed for. Before proceeding to examine the effects of price inflation it may be noted, however, that AARR's based on accelerated depreciation must be even more sensitive to growth than those based on straight-line depreciation, because the initial disparities in the net accounting rates of return for individual periods are even greater when accelerated depreciation is used. As indicated at the beginning of this section, it is precisely the fact that net accounting rates or return tend to increase from period to period under both straight-line and accelerated depreciation which explains the sensitivity of their averages to growth.

Finally, it is necessary to examine the effects of growth on $\overline{G}$. If all the f's are constant then G is also constant period to period and hence is invariant to growth. Thus, the only circumstances in which $\overline{G}$ is affected is when the f's are variable, whereas the main point of this section has been to emphasise the sensitivity of the net AARR to growth (except when economic depreciation is used) even when the f's are constant. If the f's are permitted to vary then the average value for G when investment is growing is given by

$$\overline{G} = \frac{\sum_{i=1}^{n} f_i (1+g)^{-i}}{k \sum (1+g)^{-i}} \tag{46}$$

If g=r, this simplifies to

$$\overline{G} = r\,[1 - (1+r)^{-n}]^{-1} \tag{47}$$

so that $\overline{G} \to r$ as $n \to \infty$ when g=r whatever form the sequence of f's takes. This result is the counterpart of that given in equation (42) above for the net AARR.

If the sequence of f's is declining from period to period then gross rates of return will be highest in the early periods. It follows, therefore, that $\overline{G}$ will be an increasing function of g, the rate of growth, in these circumstances and it will tend to an upper limit given by the gross rate of return in the first period, whatever that figure may be. When the f's are not constant it does not follow, of course, that $\overline{G} > r$ when there is zero growth, because a redistribution of the f's towards the early periods progressively increases r while $\overline{G}$ remains unaffected in the absence of growth. On the other hand, a declining sequence of f's tends to reduce the sensitivity of the net AARR to growth because the disparities in the net accounting rates of return for individual periods are attenuated. Indeed, if the decline is as rapid as that illustrated in Table 2.3 of the previous chapter the net $_s$AARR becomes invariant to growth because straight-line depreciation coincides with economic depreciation.

Although it is useful to establish limiting values and the ranges over which particular measures may vary, it is important not to attach exaggerated importance to the effects of growth on either the net or gross average rates of return. In practice, real rates of growth are only a few per cent per year, at least at a macro level and over long periods of time. For example, the result that the AARR=r when g=r must be treated to some extent as only a theoretical curiosity because, on average, growth rates are generally lower than internal rates of return. On the other hand, the effects of price inflation on historic cost rates of return are much more dramatic because rates of inflation have been observed to reach far higher percentages than real rates of growth, and it is necessary to turn to an examination of the effects of price changes.

Changing prices

For simplicity it will be assumed that all prices change by the same proportion so that the k and the f's belonging to the same period are all scaled up by the same factor. Inflation will also be assumed to occur at a steady rate, at least in the first instance. In order to extend and generalise the results obtained in the previous section it will be assumed that real growth takes place simultaneously with inflation. As there are interactions between the effects of growth and inflation it is necessary to allow for both at the same time.

Price changes are assumed to occur at a constant rate of 100 p per cent per period so that the price level each period is (1 + p) times that in the preceding one. Real growth will continue to be denoted by g, while growth in money, or nominal, terms will be denoted by s, which is defined as follows

$$(1+s)=(1+p)\,(1+g) \qquad (48)$$

No restrictions are imposed on the signs of p and g, either or both of which may be negative. It is usually convenient, however, to describe the process of price change as "inflation", bearing in mind that it can occasionally be negative.

The gross profits received in the current period will, of course, be at the prices of the current period and they can continue to be written as

$$F=\Sigma\, f_i\,(1+g)^{-i} \qquad (49)$$

The depreciation charges made in the current period may, however, be valued either at current prices or at the historical cost of the assets, according to the accounting convention adopted. Valuation at current prices will be referred to as current cost accounting, a procedure which leads to AARR's which are the same as those given in the previous section, where prices were assumed to be stable. The use of historic cost accounting, however, leads to very different results for depreciation, net profits and, above all, for rates of return. In the following paragraphs, the consequences of using historic cost accounting will be explored.

The depreciation charged in the current period against an investment made i periods ago needs to allow for the fact that the investment made then was not merely smaller in real terms (assuming g is positive) but was also made at lower prices. Using historic cost accounting, therefore, the depreciation currently charged in respect of an investment i periods ago is

$$d_i\,(1+g)^{-i}\,(1+p)^{-i}=d_i\,(1+s)^{-i} \qquad (50)$$

and the total of depreciation charges made in the current period is given by

$$D=\sum_{i=1}^{n}\left[d_i\,(1+g)^{-i}\,(1+p)^{-i}\right]=\sum_{i=1}^{n} d_i\,(1+s)^{-i} \qquad (51)$$

Similarly, the book value of assets at historic costs at the beginning of the current period is given by

$$K=\sum_{i=1}^{n}\left\{\left(k-\sum_{x=1}^{i} d_{x-1}\right)(1+s)^{-i}\right\} \qquad (52)$$

This equation is formally identical to equation (37) and can similarly be simplified to

$$K=\frac{1}{s}\left\{k-\sum_{i=1}^{n} d_i\,(1+s)^{-i}\right\} \qquad (53)$$

$$\text{or } K=\frac{k-D}{s} \qquad (54)$$

assuming $s \neq 0$. On re-arrangement this gives

$$\frac{k - D}{K} = s \qquad (55)$$

These expressions are generalisations of the corresponding equations (39) and (40) of the previous section. It is important to notice that D in equations (54) and (55) is defined by equation (51) above. This definition of D *replaces* that given in (36) above. Alternatively, (36) can now be regarded as a special case of (51) in which $p = 0$. The whole analysis of this section hinges on the definition of D given in (51), which implies that the depreciation charged in the current period when historic cost accounting is used is less than it would be if there were no price inflation (or if current cost accounting were used).

Equation (55) shows that the rate of growth of the capital stock measured at current prices is equal to the nominal rate of growth s whatever the sequence of f's or depreciation formula used, so long only as the formula is applied consistently to all assets. Of course, (55) reduces to (40) above when $p = 0$ so that $s = g$.

The average net rate of return using historic cost accounting is given by

$$AARR = \frac{F - D}{K} = \frac{s(F - D)}{k - D} \qquad (56)$$

where F and D are defined as in (49) and (51) while k is defined in (54). Once again a special case of considerable interest occurs when all of the gross profits earned each period are ploughed back as gross investment so that $k = F$. This implies that the real rate of growth g is equal to the internal rate of return, as can be seen from (49). In this case, it follows from (56) that

$$\text{if } k = F \text{ then } AARR = s \qquad (57)$$
$$\text{whereas } g = r$$

In other words, for a closed system consisting of a firm which systematically reinvests the whole of its gross profits, the net accounting rate of return equals its nominal rate of growth measured in money terms, whereas its real rate of growth equals its (real) internal rate of return. This result, like the corresponding one at constant prices given earlier, is quite general in that it does not depend upon any assumptions about the sequence of gross profits generated by the standard investment project nor the depreciation formula used.

When historic cost accounting is used during inflation the value of depreciation charged in the current period is reduced and net profits correspondingly increased. Although the value of net investment in the current period is also increased, the book value of total past investments is reduced by valuing them at historic cost. Thus, the numerator of an AARR based on historic cost accounting is increased by inflation while the denominator is simultaneously reduced. The effects of inflation on numerator and denominator are not self cancelling but cumulative. Not surprisingly, therefore, very high figures may be recorded for AARR's under inflation when historic cost accounting is used.

In order to appreciate the orders of magnitude involved, it is necessary to take a numerical example, and the same standard project will be used as before, namely that illustrated in Table 2.2 above. When the sequences of both the f's and the d's are constant, the expressions involving them in equation (56) may be calculated as the sums of geometric progressions, and the resulting values of the net AARR for various combinations of p and g are given in Table 3.4. The rates of inflation covered are from —10 per cent per period to +30 per cent, and the rates of growth from —10 per cent to +20 per cent.

TABLE 3.4 AARR's FOR THE ILLUSTRATIVE STANDARD INVESTMENT PROJECT UNDER DIFFERENT RATES OF REAL GROWTH AND INFLATION

Rates of price inflation p: % per period	Rates of real growth, g: % per period						
	—10	—5	Zero	5	10	15	20
30	3.352	2.066	1.379	0.996	0.772	0.634	0.544
25	2.761	1.744	1.185	0.867	0.679	0.562	0.486
20	2.194	1.429	0.993	0.739	0.586	0.490	0.427
15	1.662	1.125	0.805	0.613	0.494	0.419	0.369
10	1.179	0.838	0.622	0.488	0.402	0.347	0.310
5	0.759	0.575	0.448	0.366	0.312	0.276	0.252
Zero	0.415	0.340	0.286	0.248	0.222	0.205	0.193
−5	0.152	0.145	0.140	0.137	0.136	0.135	0.135
−10	−0.036	−0.009	0.015	0.035	0.052	0.066	0.076

Parameters of the standard investment: $n=20$, $G=0.2$, $r=0.194$. See Table 2.2.

The numerical results given in Table 3.4 illustrate the extraordinary range of AARR's which may be obtained in respect of a firm investing in a single standard project under conditions of growth and inflation. At one extreme, if both the real investment and the price level are falling by 10 per cent per period, it is impossible to cover accumulated depreciation charges out of current gross profits and the AARR is negative. On the other hand, if prices are rising by 10 per cent per period while investment is falling by 10 per cent per period, the AARR jumps to over 100 per cent. Even if p is restricted to non-negative values, rates of return ranging from just under 20 per cent to over 300 per cent are found in the table. The following generalisations may be made.

1. For any given value of g, the net AARR is a strongly increasing function of p. The *marginal* effect of p varies inversely with g and is most marked at zero or negative rates of real growth.
2. Conversely, for any given value of p, the net AARR is a decreasing function of g, provided p is non-negative. The *marginal* effect of g increases with p and is most marked at high rates of inflation.
3. When p assumes a certain negative value (about —6 per cent in this example), real growth ceases to have any effect on the AARR; for larger negative values of p, the effect of g on the AARR is reversed, the AARR becoming an increasing function of g.

Because of the kind of interactions noted in (3), it is risky to generalise from one set of numerical results, but it seems likely that, in general, high rates of inflation accentuate the effects of differences in real growth rates, whereas high rates of growth tend to dampen the effects of differences in rates of inflation. What the illustration does conclusively demonstrate is the extreme sensitivity of net AARR's based on historic cost accounting to differing rates of inflation and growth.

Before examining the further implications of these results, it is worth emphasising that they are based on the assumption of steady rates of change in both investment and prices over long periods. The net AARR's are, in effect, equilibrium values which are themselves constant from one period to the next assuming that the parameters of the underlying standard investment project remain unchanged and that rates of change remain steady. The value of gross investment at current prices is, by assumption, growing at the rate of s per period where $s=g+p\,(1+g)$; it follows that gross profits grow at the same rate. Similarly, the values of depreciation and net profits also grow at the rate s. As compared with current cost accounting, the effect of historic cost accounting is to reduce the *level* of depreciation charged and to increase the *level* of net profits each period. The proportionate *rates of change* of depreciation and net profits from period to period are the *same,* however, under both systems of accounting and equal to s. Indeed, at current prices, the values of all variables—profits both gross and net, investment, depreciation, the book value of assets—grow at the same rate s under the conditions stipulated. For this reason, any ratio of one to another, such as the AARR itself, remains constant from period to period.

CURRENT VERSUS HISTORIC ACCOUNTING

As all variables grow at the same rate whichever method of accounting is used, it may be asked what is the real objection to the use of historic cost accounting in the context of the kind of steady growth models considered in the previous section. The answer lies in the financing of the growing investment. Before investigating this matter further, it is necessary to examine more closely the relative sizes of depreciation, net profits, book values of assets and rates of return under historic and replacement cost accounting respectively.

Data based on the same illustrative standard investment project as that in Table 3.4 will be used to indicate relative orders of magnitude under different conditions. As the current period is also the base period, depreciation at current cost at different rates of real growth is given simply by choosing those values for which p=0; the ratio of depreciation at historic cost to that at current cost is therefore given by the following expression:

$$\frac{\sum d_i\ (1+s)^{-i}}{\sum d_i\ (1+g)^{-i}} \qquad (58)$$

The ratio depends on the assumed values of s, g and n, and Table 3.5 shows a selection of ratios for a constant value of n=20 for the same combinations of p and g as were used in Table 3.4.

TABLE 3.5 DEPRECIATION AT HISTORIC COST AS A PERCENTAGE OF DEPRECIATION AT CURRENT COST

(*Based on the Illustrative Standard Investment Project*)

Rate of real growth g %	Rate of price inflation *p* (%)								
	—10	—5	Zero	5	10	15	20	25	30
20	201.6	136.0	100	78.2	63.9	54.0	46.6	41.1	36.7
15	227.1	143.0	100	75.2	59.7	49.4	42.0	36.5	32.3
10	261.5	152.8	100	71.5	54.7	43.9	36.6	31.3	27.3
5	306.4	164.8	100	67.2	48.9	37.8	30.6	25.6	21.9
Zero	361.3	179.0	100	62.3	47.6	31.3	24.3	19.8	16.6
−5	422.9	194.3	100	57.4	36.3	25.1	18.5	14.4	11.7
−10	485.5	209.5	100	52.8	30.8	19.7	13.6	10.0	7.8

Parameters of the standard investment: n=20, G=0.2, r=0.194. See Table 2.2.

The data once again exhibit some interaction between p and g. The faster the rate of price inflation, the lower the ratio of depreciation at historic cost to that at current cost, as expected, but the differences are less pronounced at high rates of growth. The fall in the ratio as p increases is nevertheless quite considerable, whatever the rate of the growth. For example, when prices are rising at 10 per cent per period depreciation at historic cost is less than a half that at current cost, unless growth is fairly rapid.

Because the ratios depend only on p, g and n, it is possible to investigate the effects of variations in n by holding g constant, and a selection of ratios for different values of n are given in Table 3.6 when g=0. The row in this table where n=20 is identical, therefore, with that in Table 3.5 where g=0. The data show just how fast the ratio of depreciation at historic cost to that at current cost falls as n increases. Obviously, the distinction between historic and current cost accounting increases considerably in importance as the duration of the investment project lengthens and the data underline this fact.

The next step is to examine the ratio of net profits at historic cost to net profits at current cost at different rates of real growth and inflaion, and illustrative data are given in Table 3.7. The ratios tend to increase as inflation increases but towards upper limits. Historic cost accounting reduces depreciation, the faster the rate of inflation and the slower the rate of real growth, but is can never fall below zero, so that there is a maximum for net profits which is determined by the size of gross profits. This in turn implies that there is a maximum for the ratio of net profits at historic cost to net profits at current cost which is given by the ratio $\frac{f}{f-d}$ which happens to equal 133.3 per cent for the illustrative investment project.

TABLE 3.6 DEPRECIATION AT HISTORIC COST
AS A PERCENTAGE OF DEPRECIATION AT CURRENT COST
(Assuming Zero Real Growth)

Number of periods	Rate of price inflation *p* %						
	Zero	5	10	15	20	25	30
5	100	86.6	75.8	67.0	59.8	53.8	48.7
10	100	77.2	61.4	50.2	41.9	35.7	30.9
15	100	69.2	50.7	39.0	31.2	25.7	21.8
20	100	62.3	47.6	31.3	24.3	19.8	16.6
25	100	56.4	36.3	25.9	19.8	15.9	13.3
30	100	51.2	31.4	21.9	16.6	13.3	11.1
35	100	46.8	27.6	17.8	14.3	11.4	9.5

TABLE 3.7 NET PROFITS AT HISTORIC COST
AS A PERCENTAGE OF NET PROFITS AT CURRENT COST
(Based on the Illustrative Standard Investment Project)

Rate of real growth *g* (%)	Rate of price inflation *p* %								
	—10	—5	Zero	5	10	15	20	25	30
20	66.1	88.0	100	107.3	112.0	115.3	117.8	119.6	121.1
15	57.6	85.6	100	108.3	113.4	116.9	119.3	121.1	122.6
10	46.2	82.4	100	109.5	115.1	118.7	121.1	122.9	124.2
5	31.2	78.4	100	111.7	117.0	120.7	123.1	124.8	126.0
Zero	12.9	73.7	100	112.6	119.1	122.9	125.2	126.7	127.8
−5	−7.6	68.6	100	114.2	121.1	125.0	127.2	128.5	129.4
−10	−28.5	63.5	100	115.7	123.1	126.8	128.8	130.0	130.7

Parameters of the standard investment: n=20, G=0.2, r=0.194. See Table 2.2.

The very large variation in AARR's which can be observed in Table 3.4 cannot, therefore, be mainly attributable to variations in net profits under historic cost accounting but to variations in the book values of assets by which they are divided. The relative sizes of assets under historic and current cost accounting are given for the illustrative investment project in Table 3.8. The general pattern displayed is very similar to that for the ratios of depreciation given in Table 3.5. The ratios for book values of assets are not quite so sensitive to differing rates of inflation as those for depreciation, but they still tend to fall sharply as the rate of inflation increases: for example, with zero growth, the value of book assets at historic cost is only about a half that based on current cost when p = 10 per cent. When real growth is positive, the impact of inflation is lessened, but if real growth is negative (which happens for individual firms, or industries) the impact of inflation is very strong indeed.

The financing of investment

In the underlying model investment is assumed to grow in real or money terms at various specified rates from period to period. These growth rates are, in effect, exogenous and no consideration has so far been given to the feasibility of financing these rates of investment out of accumulated depreciation provisions, retained profits or other sources of funds.

Each period the firm withholds out of gross profits a certain amount for depreciation. The difference between this amount and the total amount needed to finance gross investment has to be found from other sources—retained profits, additional borrowing or new equity capital. In order to appreciate the financial requirements of net investment (i.e. gross investment less depreciation) they must be measured relatively to other flows and it is, therefore, proposed to examine the size of the ratio of net investment to net profits under different rates of real growth and inflation. As all the relevant variables—K, D and F—grow at the same rate in money terms along the same equilibrium growth path, as previously explained, any ratio derived from them is constant from period to period.

TABLE 3.8 BOOK VALUES OF ASSETS AT HISTORIC COST AS PERCENTAGES OF BOOK VALUES AT CURRENT COST

(Based on the Illustrative Investment Project)

Rate of real growth g (%)	Rate of price inflation p (%)								
	—10	—5	Zero	5	10	15	20	25	30
20	168.2	126.3	100	82.3	69.8	60.4	53.3	47.6	43.0
15			100						
10	197.0	135.3	100	78.1	63.6	53.4	45.9	40.3	35.8
5			100						
Zero	248.8	150.4	100	71.8	54.7	43.6	36.0	30.6	26.5
−5			100						
−10	333.2		100						16.2

Parameters of the standard investment: $n=20$, $G=0.2$, $r=0.194$. See Table 2.2.

The ratio of net investment to net profits is tabulated in Table 3.9 for the standard investment project. This ratio, which will be denoted by V, is given by

$$V=\frac{k-D}{F-D}=\frac{s}{AARR} \tag{59}$$

When there is neither real growth nor price inflation g, p and s are all zero. Gross investment k is equal to total depreciation provisions D, whatever accounting method or depreciation method is employed, so that V equals zero. This is, of course, the case of a balanced set of projects. Taking this as a point of departure, V increases as g increases reaching a value of unity (or 100 per cent in Table 3.9) when $g=r$, whatever value p assumes. As already explained, this corresponds to the case of a firm that continually re-invests the whole of its gross profits each period (i.e. $k=F$). In this case, net profits are also bound to equal net investment whatever accounting method or depreciation formula is used and whatever the rate of inflation. In Table 3.9, all the entries in the row corresponding to a real rate of growth of 19.4 per cent, the internal rate of rate, would be equal to 100 per cent. For growth rates above r the effect of p on V changes sign. When $g < r$, $D < k < F$ so that $\frac{k - D}{F - D}$ increases as p increases because D decreases. However, if $g > r$ so that $k > F$, then $D < F < k$ and $\frac{k - D}{F - D}$ decreases as p increases. This kind of interaction has already been noted earlier.

In practice, growth rates below r are the relevant ones. In this range, V increases with p, but at a diminishing rate, and approaches an upper limit. As $p \to \infty$, $D \to 0$ using historic cost accounting so that $V \to \frac{k}{F}$ which is itself an increasing function of g because the ratio of gross investment to gross profits must increase as growth increases. These limiting values for V are given in Table 3.9 for the illustrative investment project. It is useful to compare them with the values of V when $p=0$, because the latter correspond to those that would be obtained if current cost accounting were used; the differences steadily decline as g increases, from which it may be concluded once again that the importance of inflation diminishes as real growth increases. In general, the faster the rate of real growth, the lower the average age of the capital assets and hence the smaller the differences betwen the results obtained by using historic and current cost accounting respectively.

It is now necessary to consider the further implications of these results. Consider, for example, the case shown in Table 3.9 where $g=0$ and $p=15$ per cent. Using historic cost accounting the value of V is 18.6 per cent which implies

TABLE 3.9 GROSS INVESTMENT LESS DEPRECIATION AS A PERCENTAGE OF GROSS PROFITS LESS DEPRECIATION: HISTORIC COST ACCOUNTING BASED ON ILLUSTRATIVE INVESTMENT PROJECT

Rate of real growth *g* (%)	Rate of price inflation *p* %									Limiting value as $p \to 00$
	—10	—5	Zero	5	10	15	20	25	30	
20	105.4	104.1	103.6	103.3	103.2	103.1	103.0	103.0	102.9	102.7
15	53.4	68.7	73.2	75.2	76.3	77.5	77.5	77.9	78.1	79.9
10	−19.2	33.2	45.0	49.7	51.1	53.6	54.6	55.2	55.7	58.7
5	−155.8	−1.8	20.2	28.0	31.8	33.9	35.2	36.0	36.7	40.1
Zero	−575.7	−35.7	0	11.2	16.1	18.6	20.1	21.1	21.8	25.0
−5	—	−67.3	−14.7	−0.4	5.4	8.2	9.8	10.8	11.4	14.0
−10	—	−95.4	−24.1	−7.2	0.8	2.1	3.6	4.5	5.1	6.9

Parameters of the standard investment: $n=20$, $G=0.2$, $r=0.194$. See Table 2.2.

that the firm needs an amount equal to 18.6 per cent of its net profits to add to its depreciation provisions in order to have sufficient funds to maintain its gross investment as the same level as in previous periods—in other words, to maintain its real capital intact. Moreover, the firm has to raise this additional 18.6 per cent period after period in order to maintain its production at a constant level in real terms. The first possibility open to the firm is to retain 18.6 per cent of its net profits each period as corporate saving and to use these funds to supplement the inadequate depreciation provisions. The necessity to resort to this procedure, however, undermines the concept of net profit. It is precisely the fact that these funds are not in reality available to the firm for any other purpose than maintaining its real capital intact which argues that they should have been treated as costs of production and included in depreciation in the first place. Systematically retaining a proportion of net profits in this way is to practise current cost accounting in all but name. Alternatively, if the firm pays out the whole of its so-called net profits to its shareholders and borrows 18.6 per cent of them back again each period, the result is exactly the same in practice as retaining them as corporate savings in the first place, both from the point of view of the firm and its shareholders.

If, for whatever reason, the firm is financed entirely out of equity capital, one or other of the above procedures (or some combination of the two) must be employed if the firm is to maintain its real levels of investment and output, as assumed. On the other hand, if some or all of its finance is raised by a loan, the situation is different and various possibilities arise. Consider first a firm which finances the purchase of the requisite capital good each period by borrowing the whole amount of the purchase price, using subsequent depreciation provisions to pay off the loan, either in instalments or on the termination of the individual investment project, in the way described in the previous chapter. In such a case, the loan capital of the firm expressed in money terms grows at the same rate as the rate of inflation p (assuming $g=0$, as here). In principle, this is a perfectly viable growth path in money terms (or steady state in real terms). As the additional funds equal to 18.6 per cent of net profits which are needed each period are, ex hypothesi, raised by increased borrowing, the whole of the net profits calculated on the basis of historic cost accounting are at the disposal of the firm's owners in each and every period.

As explained in the previous chapter, net profits calculated on the basis of historic cost accounting can be partitioned into the operating surplus and the revaluation surplus. In the example under consideration it can be inferred that the revaluation surplus is equal to 18.6 per cent of net profits while the operating surplus accounts for the other 81.4 per cent. The two polar cases considered above of 100 per cent equity finance and 100 per cent loan finance may give the impression that the revaluation surplus is unrealised in the former case and realized in the latter. This would not be correct, however, as the revaluation surplus is realised in both cases, given that realisation occurs when either an asset is sold *or* is used in production. The point at issue is quite different therefore: namely, whether or not realised revaluation surpluses are distributable or disposable. When the firm is equity based these surpluses are not distributable because they are pre-empted by the purchasing power losses which the owners or shareholders suffer in respect of the funds which they have invested in their own firm: *with the passage of time these funds are no longer sufficient not merely for purposes of replacing physical assets as required but for purchasing any set of goods which they might have bought at the time they were invested in the firm.* On the other hand, when the firm is loan based, they are not pre-empted in this way and may therefore quite properly be distributed.

During a period of inflation redistributions of real wealth take place from lenders of funds (whose claims are denominated in amounts fixed in money terms) to owners of physical goods in a variety of different ways depending on the extent to which the latter are financed by the former. The problems under consideration are particular examples of this. In principle, however, redistribution has got nothing whatsoever to do with measuring the profitability of some process of production which uses a particular capital good, even though in practice the two are liable to become hopelessly entangled with each other because it is common to purchase capital (and other) goods by borrowing funds from others. If the objective is to measure *the profitability of a process of production* only the operating surplus calculated on the basis of current costs is relevant, whereas if it is intended to measure *the overall profitability of an enterprise* not merely the revaluation surpluses received in respect of its ownership of assets need to be included *but also* the purchasing power losses in respect of the funds invested in the enterprise by its owners.

To conclude this section and hopefully clarify the issues involved it is useful to consider the example of an enterprise whose policy is to rely half and half on equity and loan finance. Such an enterprise would have to retain half of the 18.6 per cent of net profits needed each period as corporate saving and borrow the other half, so that both its equity and loan capital would grow at the same rate in money terms. Suppose, however, that after being converted to the principle of current cost accounting it changes its policy and decides to retain 18.6 per cent of its net profits at historic costs each period in order to cover its production costs at current prices. Over the course of time the share of equity capital would gradually increase from 50 towards 100 per cent while the share of loan capital would tend towards zero. In real terms, the value of the loan capital, which would remain fixed in money terms, would be gradually eroded by inflation. However, the value of a loan between any two parties is inevitably eroded by inflation, a fact which has no particular connection with accounting methodology.

Alternatively, if the firm remains a staunch supporter of historic cost accounting it may decide to move in the other direction and start distributing the whole of its net profits and increasing its borrowing accordingly. In that case, the share of its loan capital will increase indefinitely. In this way, revaluation surpluses may be distributed in full each period but only by steadily increasing the gearing ratio, a policy which may of course be objectionable on other grounds. Indeed, in *real* terms all the firm would actually be doing would be distributing under the heading of revaluation surpluses part of its own equity capital each period by simultaneously increasing its loan capital in real as well as money terms. Such a policy may or may not be desirable, but at least the firm and its shareholders ought to recognise what is taking place. In general, in the kind of steady state situation under consideration, the proportion of its revaluation surplus which the firm should distribute to its shareholders should be the same as its gearing ratio unless the firm deliberately wishes to change the amount of its equity capital in real terms.

Finally, it must be noted that the above discussion has been conducted in the context of zero real growth only for simplicity. In general, the amounts put aside for depreciation are smaller under historic than current cost accounting when there is inflation. Thus, whatever the rate of growth, gross investment less depreciation is larger under historic cost accounting, and it is this figure which determines how much additional finance has to be raised. Moreover, it can be seen from Table 3.9 that, when $g < r$, this amount is not merely larger than under current cost accounting but represents a larger share of net profits (notwithstanding the fact that net profits are also larger under historic cost accounting). As current cost accounting is often mistakenly interpreted as accounting for replacement, it is useful to consider the example in which gross investment is declining by 10 per cent per period so that the stock of real capital is gradually run down. Under current cost accounting gross investment is less than the depreciation accruing so that the owners of firm are able to withdraw some of this capital each period. For example, using the standard investment project illustrated in Table 3.9, when g= — 10 per cent, the owners are able to withdraw an amount equal to 24.1 per cent of net profits calculated at current costs. However, if inflation is running at +15 per cent per period and historic cost accounting is used, the understatement of depreciation is so great that *an additional amount of finance equal to 2.1 per cent of net profits has to be raised each period even though in real terms capital is being run down.* Once again, this illustrates how, during inflation, net profits at historic cost contain an element which represents a withdrawal of capital in real terms. This may or may not be desirable, depending on the extent to which the firm has managed to benefit from transfers of real capital from others during inflation, *but such withdrawals should never be mistaken for profits arising from productive activity.*

Rates of return at historic costs

The above discussion has concentrated on the difficulties created when net profits are overstated because current costs of production are understated. Profits are only one of the two components which make up a rate of return and, as already indicated, the extent to which the current of value of assets may be understated by the use of historic costs is more serious than the overstatement of profits. It is difficult to know what meaning can be attached to a measure of capital which is obtained by aggregating a series of investments each of which is measured at a different set of prices. A fortiori, it is not possible to attach any meaning to rates of return which are based on historic costs, and there seems no point in calculating statistics which can only be described as grossly biased and distorted if they are interpreted as throwing any light on the rate of return which may be expected from productive activity. They only serve to confuse and it would be better if their publication were prohibited on these grounds.

Finally, it may be noted that gross rates of return based on historic cost accounting are only slightly less misleading when inflation is persistent. These are much easier to interpret because they do not involve depreciation, but even so they are liable to be very seriously biased upwards because of the under-valuation of past investments. The average gross rate of return with growth and inflation is given by the following expression

$$\overline{G}=\frac{\sum f_i\,(1+g)^{-i}}{k\sum(1+s)^{-i}} \qquad (60)$$

When the f's are constant this becomes

$$\overline{G}=G\,\frac{\sum(1+g)^{-i}}{\sum(1+s)^{-i}} \qquad (61)$$

while when g=0 it becomes

$$\overline{G}=\frac{nG}{\sum(1+p)^{-i}}=\frac{npG}{1-(1+p)^{-n}} \qquad (62)$$

Values of $\overline{G}$ can easily be tabulated for different combinations of p and g, but they will not be given because the uselessness of rates of return based on historic cost accounting when inflation is serious has already been demonstrated. The values of $\overline{G}$ tend to be lower than those of the AARR but they can still be very large: for example, values of $\overline{G}$ when $g=0$ tend to be about 20 to 30 per cent less than those for the AARR given in Table 3.4, but even $\overline{G}$ exceeds unity when $p=25$ per cent on an investment with an underlying rate of return of only 0.194.

Accelerating rates of growth and inflation

The effects of real growth and inflation on average accounting rates of return analysed in previous sections were based on the assumption of steady rates of growth or inflation. It is not possible to undertake any systematic analysis of varying rates of growth or inflation because the number of possible variations that might be envisaged is unlimited. Nevertheless, the implications of continuous acceleration, or deceleration, in rates of growth or inflation are fairly straightforward, and they will be considered in this section. The situation experienced by most countries from the mid 1960's to the mid 1970's was one of decelerating growth and accelerating inflation, and it is useful to see in what ways the conclusions reached in earlier sections would have to be modified with this pattern of events.

Net rates of return will be considered first as these are the most commonly used. It will be recalled that the net AARR is a weighted average of the individual ARR's for each of the investment projects undertaken in the past which still survive, the weights being the written down values of those investments. As the individual ARR's tend, in practice, to be lowest at the start of a project and much higher towards the end (assuming straight-line or accelerated depreciation as explained earlier in this chapter) it is clear that growth tends to reduce the net AARR because the weights attached to the youngest projects are increased. A fortiori, accelerating growth increases the weights even more so that accelerating growth tends to yield lower net AARR's than an equal amount of growth, *on average,* at a steady rate. Conversely, of course, decelerating growth tends to yield larger net AARR's than steady growth. It should be noticed, however, that *any* growth, whether accelerating or decelerating, will tend to yield a *lower* net AARR than that for a balanced set of projects, but the extent of the reduction depends on whether the rate of growth has been increasing or decreasing. It is only when growth has been negative (as distinct from positive but decelerating) that the net AARR will tend to exceed that for a balanced set of projects.

Assuming historic cost accounting is used, the effects of accelerating inflation may be inferred in a similar way. Accelerating inflation tends to reduce the measured value of the current net capital stock to an even greater extent than a steady rate of inflation. Compare, for example, a situation in which the price increase in each of the two previous periods $(t-1)$ and $(t-2)$ was 5 per cent with one in which there was no increase in $(t-2)$ and a 10 per cent increase in $(t-1)$. In the former case, the values of investments made in $(t-2)$ are about 10 per cent below current values and those in $(t-1)$ only 5 per cent below. On the other hand, in the latter case the values of investments in both $(t-1)$ and $(t-2)$ are 10 per cent below current values. In this way, inflation which has accelerated in the recent past reduces the values of all previous investments by an even greater amount than an equal cumulative amount of inflation at a steady rate. Inflation in the period immediately preceding the current one affects the valuation of all past investments and not merely the investment undertaken in that period. If it is greater than the average for earlier periods it has more effect on the valuation of the net capital stock than a burst of inflation in the more distant past. Thus, the value of the net capital stock at historic cost is much more sensitive to recent inflation than earlier rates of inflation, and it may be inferred that net AARR's at historic cost are likely to be very seriously biassed upwards as an immediate consequence of a sharp acceleration of inflation. The bias tends to be much greater than that resulting from a prolonged period of creeping inflation.

The slowing down of real growth and the acceleration of inflation observed in many countries in the early and mid 1970's would both tend to increase net AARR's based on historic cost, *ceteris paribus*. Such increases would be totally spurious, of course, and quite unrelated to real rates of return of investment. In practice, the effects of the acceleration of inflation may be presumed to have been much greater than those of the deceleration of growth, because the percentage rates of change involved were much greater. Moreover, these effects tended to obscure the fact that real rates of return were also falling at the same time in many countries, as shown in Chapter 6. It must be concluded that the information conveyed by rates of return based on historic cost was liable to be highly misleading at the time with the effects of rapidly accelerating inflation counter balancing, and thereby concealing, the deterioration in real rates of return.

When inflation decelerates, as it has done in most countries, the upward bias in rates of return at historic cost is considerably reduced. Thus, the rate of return will be lower with 10 per cent inflation in (t — 2) and zero inflation in (t — 1) than with 5 per cent inflation in both (t — 2) and (t — 1). However, it is important to note that the achievement of price stability does not eliminate the bias in historic costs rates of return so long as there are capital assets still in use which were affected by inflation at any time during their life times. As some capital assets have service lives stretching over several decades, the effects of inflation do not work their way out of the system for very many years indeed. Thus, the inflation of the 1970's will continue to distort historic cost rates of return for decades, no matter how successful countries are in containing inflation in the future. On the other hand, of course, a systematic revaluation of all existing assets to current prices will eliminate the distortions in accounting rates of return at a stroke, if price stability is achieved.

Turning to average gross rates of return, it may be inferred that they are generally much less sensitive than net rates to accelerating or decelerating real growth simply because they are less sensitive to growth itself. A priori, it is difficult to deduce much without knowing the pattern typically followed by the sequences of gross profits generated by investments. However, the value of the gross capital stock at historic cost is likely to be at least as sensitive as the net stock to recent variations in rates of price inflation because the values of assets acquired long ago and nearing the ends of their useful lives are not written down. Thus, gross rates of return at historic cost are likely to be affected by accelerating or decelerating rates of inflation in much the same way as net rates. The same conclusions may be drawn as those just reached above, which do not therefore need to be repeated.

A postscript on stock appreciation

It is necessary to conclude this chapter by pointing out that the analysis of the effects of inflation on accounting rates of return at historic costs has been exclusively concerned with the under-valuation of the capital stock and the depreciation figures derived therefrom. No account has been taken of the effects of inflation on the costs of consuming non-durable goods when historic cost accounting is used. These costs are also likely to be seriously under-estimated when there is rapid inflation, depending on the quantities of goods held in stock and the length of time they are held in stock, on average. The excess of profits at historic costs over those at current costs which is attributable to the under-statement of the current costs of consuming non-durable goods is generally referred to as "stock appreciation". This phenomenon, which affects gross profits just as much as net profits, is examined separately in Chapter 5 below. It is sufficient here to note that stock appreciation, which is clearly a type of revaluation surplus, has in practice to be added to the revaluation surpluses recorded in respect of capital goods and that it may well equal or even exceed the latter in size. Thus, accounting rates of return at historic cost are liable to be inflated even more by rising prices than the analysis of this chapter suggests. The end of the story has not been reached.

Appendix

CONSTANT ACCOUNTING RATE OF RETURN

Let an investment of k in period 0 generate a sequence of gross profits

$$f_1, f_2, \ldots f_i, \ldots f_n$$

over the subsequent n periods. The depreciation charged each period is denoted by d_i and the cost of the initial investment is subsequently recovered in full so that

$$\sum_{i=1}^{n} d_i = k \tag{1}$$

It is required to find that pattern of depreciation provisions which will ensure that the ARR, namely

$$\frac{f_i - d_i}{v_i} \tag{2}$$

is constant for each and every period no matter what the sequence of the f's: v_i is the written down value of the initial investment at the start of period i, namely

$$v_i = k - \sum_{x=1}^{i} d_{x-1} \tag{3}$$

(where $d_o = 0$ given that production starts in period 1). The solution is obtained by induction by working backwards from the last period to the first.

In the last period, the final depreciation charge d_n has to equal v_n if the costs of the original investment are to be fully recovered in depreciation charges as required by (1). The accounting rate of return in period n, which will be denoted r, is given by

$$r = \frac{f_n - d_n}{v_n} \tag{4}$$

Given that $d_n = v_n$

$$v_n = \frac{f_n}{1+r} \tag{5}$$

so that r is *also* the rate of discount which ensures that the present value of f_n is equal to the value of v_n at the start of period n.

It is required that the accounting rate of return in period (n — 1) should equal that in period n, or

$$\frac{f_{n-1} - d_{n-1}}{v_{n-1}} = r \tag{6}$$

The recovery of costs by depreciation requires that

$$d_{n-1} + d_n = v_{n-1} \tag{7}$$

while

$$v_n = v_{n-1} - d_{n-1} \tag{8}$$

by definition.
Equations (4) to (8) together imply that

$$v_{n-1}=\frac{f_{n-1}}{1+r}+\frac{f_n}{(1+r)^2} \tag{9}$$

Thus, the constant accounting rate of return in periods (n — 1) and n is equal to the discount rate which equates the present value of f_{n-1} and f_n to the value of v_{n-1} at the start of period n — 1. Similarly, it can be shown that if the accounting rate of return in period (n — 2) is to be equal to that in periods (n — 1) and n, it must also equal the discount rate applying at the start of period (n — 2), and so on back to the beginning of period 1, the start of the project. At this point the condition

$$v_1=\sum_{i=1}^{n} d_i=k$$

is added to ensure that the discount rate r is equal to the internal rate of return on the project as a whole.

It follows, therefore, that if the accounting rate of return is constant throughout every single period of the project it must be equal to the internal rate of return[1]. In general,

$$\frac{f_i - d_i}{v_i}=r \tag{10}$$

where r is defined by the equation

$$k=\sum_{i=1}^{n} f_i\,(1+r)^{-i} \tag{11}$$

The required amount to be charged as depreciation each period is therefore obtained by re-arranging (10), namely

$$d_i=f_i - rv_i \tag{12}$$

which is "economic depreciation" as defined in this paper. It is well known that the use of economic depreciation is a sufficient condition for obtaining an accounting rate of return which is constant from period to period and equal to the internal rate of return. This note shows that it is also a necessary condition for a constant accounting rate of return.

1. A different proof which uses continuous time instead of discrete accounting periods is given by J.A. Kay in "The Accountant's Rate of Profit and the Internal Rate of Return", *Oxford Economic Papers,* Vol. 28, p. 449.

Chapter 4

PROFITS AND THE OPERATING SURPLUS IN THE SNA

INTRODUCTION

National accounts are the principal source of data for macro-economic analysis, and it is inevitable that studies of profits, profitability and rates of return on capital at a macro level should be based mainly on national accounts. Each country publishes its own accounts which vary considerably from country to country in format and degree of detail shown, but underlying them all is a common basic methodology. Over the last few decades countries have tried to improve and standardise the concepts and methodology which they use, and the international organisations, notably the UN, the OECD and the EEC, have actively encouraged this process by providing the facilities which make international co-operation possible. Thus, the present SNA may be taken as the standard or norm for purposes of national accounting. Actually, a number of countries have aligned their own national accounts system with the SNA and deviate from it only with regard to presentation or some minor conceptual differences. Moreover, the national accounts data collected and published by the OECD are always adjusted to SNA definitions in principle.

The SNA has been designed by economists specifically for purposes of macro-economic analysis. While the concepts which have been developed may not be ideal for all purposes, they have been derived from basic economic principles. For example, the concept of cost is that of opportunity cost at the time a good is used, as distinct from historic cost which measures the price actually paid for some good (possibly long before it is used). The concepts and methodology in the SNA have not been constrained by factors such as administrative convenience, historical tradition, company law or tax authorities. The fact that current opportunity cost can be difficult to calculate (or perhaps one should say estimate) during inflation is tacitly treated as irrelevant. Moreover, the fact that any attempt to calculate profits on the basis of current opportunity costs may be quite unacceptable for tax purposes (or even illegal) in some countries is quietly ignored. For these reasons, data derived from business accounts or other records sometimes have to be subjected to quite substantial transformations before they are converted into a form which is suitable for the SNA.

As already mentioned, the term "profit" does not actually appear in the SNA. The operating surplus is, however, one of the more fundamental SNA concepts, and it corresponds to that of the operating profit, or trading profit, in business accounts. It measures the surplus accruing in respect of real processes of production undertaken by the firm. In a world in which prices are stable, the differences between the operating surplus in the SNA and the operating or trading profit as it is generally understood in business accounts appear to be trivial. Important differences only begin to occur in practice when prices are changing as a result of the different valuation principles adopted. When historic costs are used business profits include a revaluation surplus as well as the operating surplus, as explained earlier in this report.

Another difference which is really a matter of presentation than substance concerns the treatment of the net income which an enterprise receives from its ownership of assets, both financial and non-financial. Having calculated the operating profit, it is customary for an enterprise also to present a total profit figure which takes account of income from all sources and which also constitutes the enterprise's income or profit for tax purposes. In arriving at total profits it is customary to deduct any payments of interest or rent which the enterprise itself is obliged to make to others in respect of its loan capital or rented land. Total profits are calculated *net* of any such payments of interest or rent received or made by the firm. Thus, although such payments are strictly negative income flows their impact is for all practical purposes indistinguishable from that of actual costs of production when calculating an enterprise's total profit. They are usually deductible for tax purposes which also makes them equivalent to costs from a tax point of view. They are, of course, compulsory payments which the enterprise cannot avoid and there may perhaps be a tendency loosely to identify them with costs of production.

In the SNA a clear distinction is made between productive activities and processes by which income or wealth is distributed or redistributed. All payments of interest and rent on land are treated as distributive transactions which cannot possibly be interpreted as if they were costs of production. Having obtained the enterprise's operating surplus as the balancing item in its production account, the next account in the SNA, the income and outlay account, records all flows of income from the ownership of property *gross,* so that the enterprise's total profit in a business sense is not shown explicitly as a separate item. All the information required to calculate total profits is, however, given in the income and outlay account, so that the difference between business and national accounting in this respect is essentially a matter of presentation rather than substance. Conversely, an enterprise's total income in the SNA has to be distinguished from its total profits in a business sense, because total income is shown gross while payments of interest and rent are treated as appropriations out of that total gross income alongside other appropriations such as taxes and dividends.

The document in which the SNA is described[1] is a complex volume which is not easy reading for anyone not already thoroughly familiar with the principles of national accounting. In many ways, it is a reference book for the expert rather than an expository text for the general economist or accountant. Moreover, if one is interested in the treatment of only a single item, such as the operating surplus, it is not easy to find a comprehensive explanation of it when references to the item may be scattered throughout the volume. Accordingly, the purpose of the present chapter is to bring together the various parts of the SNA which are relevant to the operating surplus and to provide a complete self-contained description of the concept. Some acquaintance with basic economic concepts such as value added is presumed, but otherwise it is intended that the contents of this chapter should be self-explanatory. It is not proposed to dwell on the minutiae of national accounting, such as the treatment of net casualty insurance premiums or imputed social security contributions whose explanation is tiresomely time consuming in relation to their importance. In the interests of simplicity attention will be focussed on the main items in the following sections. It is always possibly to consult the original SNA for a detailed explanation of the various minor miscellaneous items referred to below.

Finally, it may be noted that the system of national accounts elaborated by the European Economic Communities, namely the *European System of Integrated*

1. United Nations, *A System of National Accounts,* Studies in Methods, Series F, No. 2, Rev. 3 (New York, 1968).

Economic Accounts or ESA, is broadly consistent with the SNA. It has indeed been described as the Communities' "version" of the SNA tailored to suit their own requirements.

THE OPERATING SURPLUS IN THE SNA[2]

The definition of the operating surplus

The operating surplus of an enterprise or producer unit is equal to its value added *minus* the sum of:

1. Compensation of employees.
2. Indirect taxes paid by the producer *less* subsidies received and
3. Consumption of fixed capital.

As defined, therefore, the operating surplus is net of capital consumption, and in the absence of any other qualification it must be presumed to be net. On the other hand, there does not appear to be any major objection to re-introducing the terms "gross" and "net", and in the context of this report and also in the interests of clarity it is necessary to be quite explicit as to whether the operating surplus is gross or net of capital consumption. The traditional terminology is used in the ESA where the distinction between the gross and net operating surplus is retained.

As the concept of the operating surplus is derived from that of value added it is necessary to examine the concept of value added in more detail.

Value added

Value added is defined gross of capital consumption and in the absence of any qualification must be presumed to be gross. As in the case of the operating surplus, however, there is no objection in principle to re-introducing the terms gross and net in the interests of clarity.

There is more than one concept of value added in the SNA, however, depending upon the prices at which gross output and intermediate inputs are valued. Unfortunately, there are no less than six methods of valuation specified in the SNA, but in practice only three at most are relevant here, namely:

purchasers' values	=	valuation at the prices actually paid in the market by the purchaser.
producers' values	=	valuation at producers' prices, i.e. ex-factory or ex-farm prices: equals purchasers' values *less* trade and transport margins.
approximate basic values (often described simply as basic values)	=	valuation at producers' prices *excluding* any commodity taxes (less subsidies) levied on the output of the producer (but not other indirect taxes).

The basic values are "approximate" because any commodity taxes already paid at earlier stages of production on the intermediate inputs purchased by the producer are not excluded. (Factor, as distinct from basic, values exclude all net indirect taxes by the produced including, for example, property taxes or vehicle taxes which are not levied on the producer's output.)

The appropriate definition of value added which is implied in the definition of the operating surplus given above (and in paras. 7.10 and 7.38 of the SNA) is:

> Value added is equal to gross output at producers' values *minus* intermediate consumption at purchasers' values.

2. SNA, paras 7. 10. 7. 38.

This concept is referred to in the SNA as *value added in producers' values:* in arriving at value added at producers' values it should be noticed that the purchasers' values of intermediate inputs are subtracted from the producers' values of gross output.

Another concept of value added which is in actual use is value added in approximate basic values: this equal gross output in approximate basic values *less* intermediate inputs in purchasers' values: this obviously differs from value added in producers' values only by the amount of net commodity taxes on the producer's output.

Thus, a more detailed definition of the operating surplus in the SNA is as follows:

operating surplus (net) = the producers' values of gross output *minus* the sum of

1. The purchasers' values of intermediate consumption.
2. Compensation of employees.
3. Indirect taxes *less* subsidies and
4. Consumption of fixed capital.

Net indirect taxes here cover all indirect taxes paid less subsidies received by the producer, whether commodity taxes or not.

In order to be more precise about the concept and content of the operating surplus, it is necessary to examine in turn each of the constituent items listed above, namely, gross output, intermediate inputs, etc.

Gross output

The following refers only to the gross output of industries and does not cover producers of government services and private non-profit institutions.

Gross output is the market value of all goods and services produced within the period of account. There are three components of gross output:

goods and services sold
changes in stocks of finished goods and work in progress
goods and services produced on own account, including fixed capital formation; also income in kind supplied to employees.

Goods and services sold are valued at the time when they leave the establishment, including any indirect taxes, but excluding any trade or transport margins subsequently incurred in delivering the goods to their final purchasers. Valuation at producers' prices can equally well be described as valuation at ex-works, ex-factory or ex-farm prices.

Changes in stocks of finished goods and work in progress are valued at producers' prices, which in the case of partially processed goods means the prices which the producer would realise if they were sold in that state. The producers' prices to be used are those current at the time the changes occur.

Own-account production should also be valued at the corresponding producers' price on the market, although it is recognised that own-account fixed capital formation, especially construction, may have to be valued at costs of production.

Intermediate consumption

This includes non-durable goods and services used up in production during the period of account as well as outlays on repair and maintenance, research, development and prospecting. The commodities should be valued at the purchasers' values which are current at the moment of use.

Compensation of employees

This covers not merely wages and salaries in cash and kind, but also employers' contributions to social security schemes, private pension schemes, etc. in respect of their employees.

Indirect taxes less subsidies

Indirect taxes are levied on producers in respect of the production, sale, purchase or use of goods and services *which they charge to expenses of production.* Subsidies include all grants on *current* account which producers receive from government.

Consumption of fixed capital

This is defined as "that part of the gross product which is required to replace fixed capital used up in the process of production". It includes foreseen obsolescence, but not unforeseen obsolescence which is treated as a capital loss. Charges for the depletion of exhaustible natural resources are not included. The SNA considers it "reasonable" to value capital consumption on a straight-line basis with reference to the expected economic lifetime of the individual asset. The valuation of capital consumption is at current cost: that is, each asset should be valued at current purchasers' prices.

Charges against the operating surplus

Various compulsory or obligatory payments have to be made out of the operating surplus before arriving at a figure which in any way represents the surplus at the free disposal of the owners or managers of an enterprise. In the SNA, however, the operating surplus itself is not decomposed any further because it is carried over into the income and outlay account, where the property income of the enterprise and various minor miscellaneous current receipts are added to it before considering any appropriations out of these combined incomes.

Nevertheless, it is instructive to consider the nature of the various compulsory payments which would have to be met out of the operating surplus of an enterprise if it had no other sources of income whatsoever. The various payments which may have to be met are as follows:

rent on land
interest on long and short term debts
corporation, or income, taxes
other miscellaneous payments

In the SNA property income is treated as a *current transfer:* it is defined as a transfer of income resulting from the use by one economic agent of the land, financial assets and intangible assets, such as copyrights and patents, owned by another economic agent.

Rent

Rent in respect of land is treated as a form of property income. On the other hand, the letting of structures, equipment, machinery and other goods is considered to be a commodity type service. The rent paid in respect of these items is included in the intermediate consumption of the user (or final consumption of households). In principle, rents such as farm rents which cover buildings and equipment as well as land should be split into two parts, one of which is treated as a cost of production and the other as a transfer.

Interest

Interest is evidently a form of property income which must therefore be treated as a current transfer out of the operating surplus and not as a cost of production.

Corporation or income taxes

The distinction between direct and indirect taxes in the SNA hinges on whether or not the taxes are considered to be costs of production. Direct taxes should be recorded in SNA when they are due for payment, without penalty, as distinct from when the income was earned or when the assessment was made. In practice they are often recorded when they are actually paid or even received by government.

Other miscellaneous payments

These consist of net casualty insurance premiums, fines and penalties and unfunded employee welfare benefits.

Distributable and retained profits

In the absence of other sources of income, it would be possible to subtract from the operating surplus the various items listed above in order to arrive at a measure of "distributable profits". After deducting dividends, "retained" profits could be obtained.

In practice, neither "distributable" or "retained" profits are SNA concepts. The saving of corporate and quasi-corporate enterprises is calculated in the SNA after adding property income and other miscellaneous current receipts to the operating surplus in the Income and Outlay account. Before considering this account, it is necessary to examine the nature of the producer units.

Producer Units

An *establishment* is engaged on the production of as homogeneous a collection of goods as possible. It is owned and controlled by a single entity and it must be possible to obtain separate data in respect of production and all intermediate and primary inputs. In principle, the operating surplus of an establishment can always be calculated.

A corporate enterprise is a corporation, company, co-operative, etc., which is a business entity which exists independently of its owners.

A quasi-corporate enterprise is a relatively large partnership, sole proprietor-ship or government enterprise which has a complete set of accounts.

An *unincorporated enterprise* is, therefore, a relatively small sole proprietorship or partnership consisting typically of self-employed proprietors with few employees, and perhaps relying on unpaid family workers.

There is no simple or clear criterion whereby a quasi-corporate enterprise can be distinguished from an unincorporated one. The extent to which enterprises are incorporated varies from country to country for legal or tax reasons, and the intention of introducing the concept of the quasi-corporate enterprise was to reduce the impact of these institutional effects by treating large unincorporated businesses, which in most countries would be incorporated, as quasi-corporate and then grouping them with the corporate enterprises. It is doubtful how successfully this intention has been realised. There seems to be some reluctance, at least in some countries, to classify even quite large unincorporated enterprises as quasi-corporate. Unfortunately, therefore, the border line between corporate and quasi-corporate enterprises, on the one hand, and unincorporated enterprises on the other, cannot be presumed to be determined by the use of the exactly same criteria in different countries.

An enterprise may, of course, own and control several different establishments. An industrial classification of enterprises on the basis of their principal activity does not yield the same results as an industrial classification of establishments. Provision is made in the SNA for a broad industrial classification of enterprises and the operating surplus may be tabulated according to both kinds of industrial classification.

One major feature of the SNA is the separation of the producers of government services, domestic services and the producers of private non-profit services to households from industries which are engaged on the production of goods and services to be sold at prices normally intended to cover their costs of production.

Entrepreneurial Income

The entrepreneurial income of an enterprise is the sum of its operating surplus and its net property income. The latter is simply the difference between property income received from interest, dividends, rents and royalties and property income paid (*except* dividends in the case of corporate enterprises).

(An unincorporated enterprise is deemed not to receive any property income because any such income would accrue directly to the owner of the business in his capacity as private individual. On the other hand, property income such as interest or rent may have to be paid out in connection with the activities of the business. Thus, for an unincorporated enterprise, entrepreneurial income is the operating surplus *less* property income paid in respect of the business.)

Quasi-corporate, as well as corporate, enterprises may earn interest, rents or royalties in respect, for example, of financial assets held or land which they possess. Withdrawals from the entrepreneurial income of quasi-corporate enterprises are the analogue of the dividends paid by corporate enterprises. They represent the amounts taken by the owners of quasi-corporate enterprises out of the operating surplus and net property incomes earned by the enterprises. Not all the entrepreneurial income earned need be withdrawn so that quasi-corporate enterprises may have savings retained within the enterprises. It is possible, of course, for a quasi-corporate enterprise to be owned by a corporate enterprise so that the income of the latter may include withdrawals from the entrepreneurial income of any quasi-corporate enterprises which it owns.

Income and outlay accounts

The income and outlay accounts of the SNA are the current accounts of the institutional sectors. One of these sectors consists of non-financial corporate and quasi-corporate enterprises, a sector which may be further disaggregated on a broad industrial basis. The account appears as follows for non-financial corporate and quasi-corporate enterprises:

Current receipts	*Item*
Operating surplus (net)	1
Property income and withdrawals from entrepreneurial income of quasi-corporate enterprises, receivable	2
Casualty insurance claims receivable	3
Unfunded employee welfare contributions, imputed	4

Current disbursements	*Item*
Withdrawals from the entrepreneurial income of quasi-corporate enterprises, disbursement	5
Property income payable	
Interest	6
Rent	7
Dividends	8
Net casualty insurable premiums payable	9
Direct taxes	10
Unfunded employee welfare benefits	11
Current transfers n.e.c. net	12
Saving	13

The above account may be simplified and re-arranged. First, all the small items may be consolidated by defining a single item "net miscellaneous receipt" as equal to items (3+4) — (9+11+12). Second, items 5 and 8 may be combined and defined as "discretionary distributions": these consist of dividends paid out by corporate enterprises plus the withdrawals of entrepreneurial income from quasi-corporate enterprises. The income and outlay account may now be written as:

Current receipts	*Item*
Operating surplus	a
Property income and withdrawals from entrepreneurial income of quasi-corporate enterprises, receivable	b
Net miscellaneous receipts	c

Current disbursements	*Item*
Obligatory payments:	
Interest and rent	d
Direct taxes	e
Discretionary distributions	f
Saving	g

If the account is compiled in this form for corporate enterprises only, item f becomes simply "dividends", although item b may still possibly include some withdrawals of entrepreneurial income from quasi-corporate enterprises owned by corporate enterprises: these withdrawals will be treated below as forming part of the latter's own entrepreneurial income, although the SNA is not absolutely explicit on this point.

Two more income flows will now be defined:

first, the "total income" of corporate and quasi-corporate enterprises will be defined as the sum of items (a+b+c) above [in practice, item (c) tends to be of minor importance compared with (a) and (b)];

second, the "distributable income" of corporate and quasi-corporate enterprises will be defined as their total income minus the obligatory payments which have to be made out of it: it equals (a+b+c) — (d+e), or alternatively it equals (f+g).

The following relationships apply between the various income concepts.

Total income of corporate and quasi-corporate enterprises
minus Interest and rents paid and net miscellaneous receipts
= Entrepreneurial income (as defined in the SNA)
minus Direct taxes
= Distributable income
minus Discretionary distributions
= Saving (as defined in the SNA)

This schematic representation brings out that, working with the SNA income and outlay account, the derived or implicit concepts of "distributable income" and "saving" relate to the total incomes of corporate and quasi-corporate enterprises and not merely to their operating surpluses.

Inventory and the inventory valuation adjustment

This subject is considered at some length in a separate section. The purpose of the present note is to clarify the exact treatment of inventories in the SNA. The treatment of inventories from the side of production (as distinct from their role as an element of final demand) is embedded in the concepts and definitions of gross output and intermediate consumption respectively. It is convenient therefore to distinguish between:

i) stocks of materials or other goods bought by the establishment for further processing and

ii) work in progress and stocks of finished goods intended for sale by the establishment.

Stocks of materials not processed by the establishment

Intermediate consumption is defined as non-durable goods and services *used up* in production (italics added). The SNA focusses immediately on the goods actually fed into the production process without bothering whether they are bought in or withdrawn from stock. The goods are valued at purchasers' prices (in other words, at the cost of the items in the market at the point of delivery to the consuming establishment) *at the moment* the items enter into the production of the unit (SNA para. 6.56). This procedure constitutes valuation at current replacement cost.

It is convenient, and often appropriate, to imagine all purchases of materials being channelled into production via stocks: that is, to imagine all materials used being withdrawn from the establishment's stocks as required. The SNA then values each withdrawal at its current replacement cost as the good is used. The total value of the intermediate consumption of some good over the year is therefore equal to the total quantities used multiplied by a weighted average of the current prices, the weights being the quantities used at each price.

A business usually values intermediate consumption as total purchases within the period plus beginning of period stocks, minus end of period stocks using some conventional method of valuing those stocks. These methods are discussed in the following chapter. The difference between the value of intermediate consumption as calculated by the firm and that specified in the SNA could be considered as stock appreciation, although the concept of stock appreciation does not appear as such in the SNA as it is not needed when the various goods produced and consumed by producer units are valued according to SNA principles.

Work in progress and stocks of finished goods

Gross output is recorded in the SNA when the goods are *made,* whether they are sold, go into stock as work-in-progress or finished goods, or become part of the establishment's fixed capital formation. The output is valued at producers' prices in every case, although it is admitted that exceptions may be needed in practice for both work-in-progress and own-account capital formation which may have to be valued at cost. As in the case of intermediate consumption, there is no explicit reference to stock appreciation, although implicity it may arise when firms use different methods to value their stocks.

Increases in stocks

Increases in stocks do not appear explicitly in the production accounts of the SNA in which the operating surplus is derived, because output and intermediate consumption are defined in such a way as to make any reference to stocks unnecessary. Nevertheless, increases in stocks do appear in the capital formation accounts and it is convenient to examine this item briefly at this point.

The SNA is concerned with the *physical changes* in stocks held as distinct from their levels. If no changes in stocks occur, nothing has to be estimated or recorded. Whenever a change occurs the SNA values it at the price prevailing at that moment, using purchasers' or producers' prices depending upon whether or not the goods have already been processed internally by the establishment (as explained in previous paragraphs). The change in stocks over the period as a whole is the algebraic sum of all the positive and negative changes which occur within the period, each of which is valued separately. If, for example, stocks fall and rise back to their original level by the end of the period, the SNA will value the reduction and subsequent increase separately, so that during a period of rising prices, the overall value of the change in stocks will assume some positive figure even though the quantity of stocks is the same at the end as at the beginning.

The method to be followed in practice for measuring changes in stocks which is actually recommended in the SNA is stated to be only *approximate* (para. 6.113). This method is simply to value the net change in stocks between the beginning and end of the period at the average prices prevailing within the period. Even if prices rise at a constant arithmetic rate over the period this method does not necessarily yield the correct figure unless the changes in stocks also take place at a constant arithmetic rate. The approximation should be close, however, unless there is a marked fluctuation in the level of stocks or in prices within the period.

Capital consumption

Although capital consumption have already been discussed in great detail in the two previous chapters, it is worth indicating briefly here exactly how it is treated in the SNA. It is stated in para. 7.19:

> "Consumption of fixed capital may be defined in general terms as that part of the gross product which is required to replace fixed capital used up in the process of production during the period of account. This flow is based on the expected economic lifetime of the individual assets: and is designed to cover *the loss in value* due to foreseen obsolescence and the normal amount of accidental damage which is not made good by repair, as well as normal wear and tear." (Italics added)

The emphasis on replacement in this definition is unfortunate as there is no presumption that any particular asset is replaced in practice. Moreover, the definition is not very helpful as it gives no indication as to how the loss in value is to be measured. In order to remedy this the SNA goes on to specify in para. 7.21:

> "In a stationary economy in which the quantity of fixed assets in use remains the same and does not change in quality, consumption of fixed capital can readily be defined so that in each year it is equal to the replacement needed. The problem of definition is however more complicated in an economy characterized by changes in demand or by technical changes leading to obsolescence; and no general rule can be formulated for such situations. It seems reasonable, however, to value consumption of fixed capital on a straight-line basis with reference to the expected economic lifetime of the individual assets."

A little later, the valuation of assets at historic cost is firmly rejected. Thus, in para. 7.22 it is stated:

> "In general, producers base their methods of computing annual provisions for wear and tear and foreseen obsolescence on the concept of maintaining the money value of their capital intact by allocating the original cost of the asset over its expected economic lifetime. This procedure is open to objection since, as prices and techniques change, *the cost of using fixed assets may be greater or less than that obtained by such a calculation.* Accordingly, estimates of consumption of fixed capital should take into account the cost of replacing the assets in the period for which the estimates are being made." (Italics added)

A little later, the following observation is made about back-log depreciation in para. 7.23:

> "... no attempt should be made to allow for arrears of depreciation arising from the fact that earlier provisions have been made at a lower price level, *since the estimates of consumption of fixed capital are treated as a current cost of production.*" (Italics added)

It is conceded that, in practice, the estimation of capital consumption at current costs may be difficult so that the adjustment needed to depreciation provisions recorded by business at historic costs "may be considerable and subject to a large margin of error" (7.24). However, the estimates of capital consumption at current cost which now appear in the national accounts of an increasing number of countries are not derived by adjusting business depreciation provisions but quite independently from estimates of the capital stock at current cost compiled by the perpetual inventory method. This possibility is not considered in the SNA. As already mentioned, it seems to be fairly standard practice to use the straight-line depreciation formula to calculate estimates of the *net* capital stock by the perpetual inventory method, but estimates, of the *gross* stock, while possibly sensitive to assumptions about the lifetimes of assets, do not, of course, require any estimates of capital consumption.

Chapter 5

STOCKS AND STOCK APPRECIATION

INTRODUCTION

In general terms, stock appreciation may be described as a revaluation surplus on holdings of stocks, or inventories, of non-durable goods. This surplus forms part of the gross profits of enterprises whose accounts are compiled on the basis of historic costs. It is excluded from profits calculated at current costs and hence it does not figure in the SNA. When profits which were originally calculated at historic costs are used in national accounts it is necessary to adjust them for stock appreciation, and the size of the adjustment needed has been very large in recent years. In a few countries, the aggregate profit figures reported by companies are actually shown in the national accounts, in which case it is necessary to calculate and publish the amount by which they need to be reduced to eliminate stock appreciation. For example, the "inventory valuation adjustment" for the United States in 1974 was equal to 19 per cent of gross corporate profits and 32 per cent of net profits: it exceeded the total amount paid out in dividends and also the undistributed profits remaining. In the United Kingdom the adjustment was even larger relatively, amounting to no less than 48 per cent of the total gross trading profits of companies in 1974.

Most countries do not publish figures for stock appreciation because they do not publish any figures of gross corporate profits at historic costs. In some cases, gross corporate profits may be estimated by means of a quite different methodology; for example, operating surpluses may be estimated residually within the context of an aggregate input-output table in which the rules of current cost accounting are respected. Using this methodology there is no original figure at historic cost to be adjusted. Thus, the fact that the national accounts do not contain any item for stock appreciation usually signifies that aggregate operating surpluses are not derived directly from company accounts. It should not be interpreted as indicating that stock appreciation is not a major component of profits at historic costs as reported by businesses.

Finally, it may be observed by way of introduction that stock appreciation depends not only on the rate of price inflation but also on the accounting conventions used by businesses. For example, stock appreciation is liable to be much smaller when LIFO is practised than FIFO. In this respect, the situation is more complicated than for durable goods where there are no problems in identifying the times at which particular pieces of machinery or equipment were bought.

THE TREATMENT OF STOCKS IN THE SNA

A revaluation surplus occurs when prices change during the period of time which elapses between the purchase or production of a good and its eventual use or sale. In the calculation of the operating surplus in the SNA, however, goods are valued only at a single moment of time either when they are consumed or used in the relevant process of production or when they emanate as outputs from production. If a good which is consumed as an intermediate input is withdrawn from stock it has to be valued in the same way whether it is viewed as a stock withdrawal or as an input. Similarly, if an output is put into stock it has to be valued in the same way whether viewed as an output or as an addition to stocks.

The valuation principles adopted in the SNA are as follows:

> "Gross additions to stocks should be evaluated at purchasers' values where acquired from other economic agents, or at the producers' values where the additions have been processed internally. The purchasers' and producers' values *which are current at the time the additions are made* should be used. Similarly, stocks withdrawn for internal processing, or on sale, are to be evaluated at *current* producers' values if already processed internally, or at purchasers' values if this is not the case. Producers' values for partially processed commodities are, of course, to be assigned in terms of the prices which the given commodities would fetch on the market if sold in that state." (Italics added) (SNA, para. 6.109).

It should be noted that this method calls for an evaluation of *changes* in stocks *as they actually occur*. It does not require the level of stocks at any moment of time to be evaluated; nor does it attempt to measure changes in stocks by comparing their levels at two separate points of time, such as the beginning and end of the accounting period. It follows that the prices at which stocks of goods were originally acquired are quite irrelevant. The value of changes in stocks over a finite period of time such as a year is obtained therefore by cumulating the values of a succession of actual stock changes.

When prices are changing rapidly physical changes in stocks which occur early in the accounting period will be valued at quite different prices from similar quantitative changes occurring later in the period. In recent years, commodity prices have been known to rise by 100 per cent or more within the space of a year, while even the prices of manufactured goods have risen by up to 30 per cent within a year in some countries. Thus, price changes have been occurring within the space of a single accounting period which were previously spread over many years. In economic accounts, most discussion of price changes have focussed on the problems of making meaningful comparisons between accounts compiled for different years, but there are also difficult problems involved in interpreting the accounts for a single period of time when prices have been changing rapidly within that period. Transactions are not valued homogenously within the period, and there could conceivably be a need in some circumstances for the accounts for a single period to be recalculated at constant prices equal to those actually prevailing in the middle of the period in question, in order to isolate the impact of price changes within the period.

Changes in stocks throw these kinds of problems into sharp relief because the changes can be negative as well as positive. Levels of stocks may fluctuate considerably within the space of a year, possibly as a consequence of marked changes in prices. It is instructive, therefore, to examine the effects of fluctuations in stock levels on the values of stock changes as measured in the SNA. Regular fluctuations may occur in stocks of both materials and finished goods because of seasonal factors. When these are combined with a strongly rising trend in prices, quite significant values may be recorded for changes in stocks, even if physical stocks return to their initial levels at the end of each accounting period. Suppose, for example, a firm manufactures principally for the spring and summer season so that its stocks reach a peak at the end of December following to a low point at the end of June. Changes in stocks are negative in the first half of the year and positive in the second half; it is obvious that, assuming that the total physical change is the same in both halves, the cumulative value of the withdrawals from stock will be less than the cumulative value of the additions to stock if prices have been rising steadily throughout. The value of stock changes will be positive therefore, even though the physical change in stocks is zero between the beginning and end of the period.

Such cases can be investigated analytically by assuming that stock levels fluctuate regularly following sinusoidal functions while prices rise continuously in an exponential manner. Three cases have been analysed and they may be identified by referring to the following diagram.

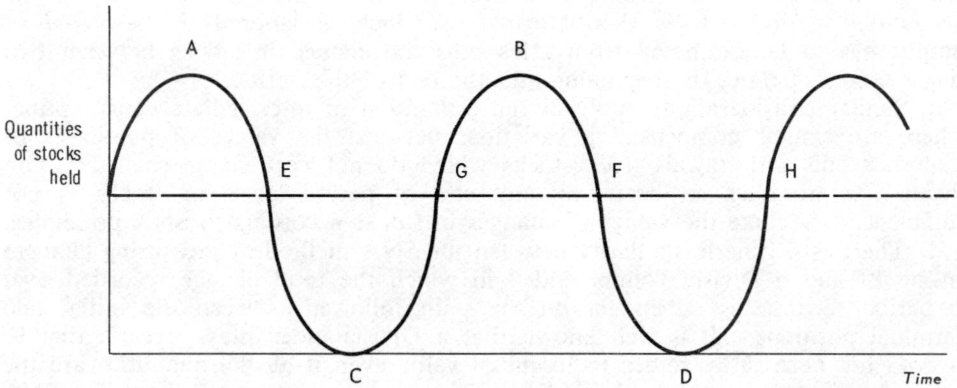

Case 1 It is assumed that the accounting period runs from A to B in the above diagram. It can be proved that the value of changes in stocks over the period as a whole (following SNA principles) as a percentage of the *average* value of stocks held throughout the period, is approximately equal to the percentage rate of inflation itself. The physical change in stocks is nevertheless zero between beginning and end of the period.

Case 2 It is assumed that the accounting period runs from C to D in the diagram. In this case, the value of the change in stocks as a percentage of the average value of stocks held is also approximately equal to the percentage rate of inflation, but *negative* in sign.

Case 3 It is assumed that the accounting period runs from E to F or from G to H. In each case, the value of the changes in stocks is approximately equal to zero, as the values of the positive and negative changes in stocks roughly cancel each other out.

Comparing cases 1 and 2 it appears odd at first that merely by switching the boundaries of the accounting period a positive value for changes in stocks can be turned into a negative value, or vice versa, when the underlying processes of production may be the same in both cases. It must be emphasised, therefore, that if production is steady in both cases (the fluctuations in stocks being attributable to seasonal variations in demand), the value of *output* will be the same in both cases. The explanation is that the difference between the values of changes in stocks must be exactly counterbalanced by an opposite difference in sales values. In case 1, sales reach a peak in the first half of the accounting period, while in case 2, sales reach a peak in the second half. Thus, other things being equal, during a period of rising prices, the value of sales will be less in case 1 than case 2. The value of output is measured by sales *plus* changes in stocks, and the sum of the two will be identical in both cases even though the two separate components differ. In effect, the value of changes in stocks is an adjustment item whereby the value of output can be derived from the value of sales. It has always been recognised that such an adjustment is necessary when there is a physical change in stocks over the period as a whole because quantities produced do not equal quantities sold. The above example shows that it may also be necessary even when the total quantities produced and sold are identical over the period as a whole if the quantities are not sold at the same rate as they are produced (when prices are changing).

These examples illustrate that the values of sales and of changes in stocks are interdependent, both being influenced by the pattern of sales within the accounting period. It is this information which is ignored if the value of output has to be estimated from sales plus the change in stocks between two single points of time, the beginning and the end of the period.

Similar considerations apply to the estimation of intermediate consumption. There are similar compensating variations between the values of purchases of materials and withdrawals from stocks which do not need to be spelled out in detail. Information on beginning and end of period levels of stocks is not sufficient to estimate the values of changes in stocks according to SNA principles.

There is a generic similarity between the SNA method of measuring changes in stocks and a Divisia volume index in which the total change recorded over a period to time is dependent on the path followed between the initial and terminal positions. It is well known that a Divisia index may "cycle"; that is, it does not necessarily return to its initial value even if all the quantities are the same at the end as at the beginning. This property is matched by the SNA measure of the value of changes in stocks not necessarily being zero even though the physical quantities of stocks return to their initial levels.

Approximate methods

While it is important to establish clearly how changes in stocks ought to be measured in principle according to the SNA, it is obvious that the data required are seldom likely to be available, requiring as they do a continuous monitoring of stock changes. Such information may perhaps be available for individual enterprises, especially if they use accounting procedures such as the "base stock method", but it is difficult to imagine it ever being available for the economy as a whole. On the contrary, changes in stocks are frequently among the least reliable items in national accounts, often being estimated residually within an input-output table.

Given the paucity of data available the method which is most commonly used to estimate changes in stocks is to take the difference between the quantities of stocks held at the beginning and end of the period multiplied by their average price within the period. Notwithstanding the possibility of situations of the kind considered in the previous section in which such an approximation might be poor, this method is generally considered to be acceptable in practice. Even the SNA itself recommends it: "The closest feasible approximation to the desired measure may be the difference between the levels of stocks at the beginning and end of the period, both valued at the appropriate average prices ruling over the period" (para. 6.113). As already indicated, the appropriate prices are purchasers' prices when the goods have been bought from others or producers' prices when the goods have been processed internally. As a further concession to practicality, the

SNA admits that it may be necessary to value goods processed internally at their unit costs rather than at producers' prices when the latter are difficult to estimate (e.g. for partially processed goods). Using SNA procedures it is not necessary to invoke any convention for dating goods held in stock, such as FIFO or LIFO, because only additions to, or withdrawals from, stocks have to be valued, and for this purpose current purchasers' or producers' prices are used.

The treatment of stocks in business accounts

There is no single method which is universally applied to measure stocks and changes in stocks in business accounting. There may be a few firms which practice a form of current cost accounting which is essentially the same as that proposed in the SNA, but the great majority of firms in all countries appear to use some form of historic cost accounting. Thus, the cost which is charged for items withdrawn from stock is the same as that recorded when they entered stock. If their current price when they are withdrawn from stock, either to be processed or sold, exceeds that when they entered stock, a revaluation surplus occurs which will be incorporated in gross profits.

It is customary in business accounting to calculate the cost of sales (that is, the intermediate costs to be matched against the value of sales receipts) as purchases of materials plus the value of beginning of period stocks minus the value of end of period stocks. The beginning of period stocks are treated as it were a purchase from the previous accounting period while the end of period stocks are treated as a sale to the next accounting period. The problem therefore is how to impute a value to the beginning and end of period stocks. It is not sufficient for this purpose to invoke the principle of historic cost accounting, because there is a second and quite distinct question to be answered: namely, precisely which goods remain in stock at the end of any given period? These must be identified before they can be valued, even when the method of valuation has been already agreed.

Where goods are unique and can be separately identified, no problem arises, but when stocks consist of many homogeneous goods such as raw materials or mass produced items, there is a genuine problem of identification which is most obvious in the example of bulk liquids. In practice, firms carry stocks of hundreds of different types of goods and it is quite impossible for each item held in stock to be traced individually. Two conventions are widely used in all countries to resolve this problem. One convention is to assume that goods are withdrawn from stock in the same order as that in which they were originally acquired, or FIFO, "first-in-first-out". The alternative is to assume that the goods withdrawn are those acquired most recently, or LIFO, "last-in-first-out". Neither assumption may be realistic. It is probable that FIFO approximates the more closely to the actual order of events in most circumstances, but there are other cases where LIFO is a better approximation—e.g. when goods are stored in bins which are filled and emptied from the top. However, the choice between FIFO and LIFO is seldom made on grounds of realism but on grounds of administrative convenience, or to gain tax advantages. For this reason, the objectivity of historic cost accounting is somewhat illusory. Although previous prices may be historic facts, the wrong prices may be applied to the goods held in stock.

It is necessary to examine the implications of FIFO and LIFO separately, as the amount of stock appreciation which gets included in the profits of any given period is usually quite different under the two systems. On the other hand, as these topics are dealt with extensively in various other publications, it is not proposed to go into much detail here.

FIFO

In practice, when FIFO is used for purposes of valuing stocks it is usually combined with the principle that stocks should be valued at historic cost or current market value, whichever is the lower. During a period of general price inflation in which individual prices seldom fall, even if they may remain stationary for a time, this method of valuation generally implies historic costs.

Consider an example in which the stocks consist of intermediate goods which are typically held by a firm for three months before being used. For simplicity, it will be assumed that both purchases of materials and their use in production proceed at the same rate throughout the year so that the physical quantities of stocks held remain constant. With stocks turning over once every three months, the materials fed into production during the accounting year January to December will, under FIFO, be deemed to be those purchased during the twelve months October to September which precede the accounting year by three months. The materials purchased during the nine months January to September which are common to both years are charged as costs of production within the accounting year at their current prices. The materials purchased in the last three months of the accounting year are not treated as costs at all because they are deemed not to be used within the year: they are treated as if they were sold again, at their historic costs, to the subsequent accounting year. The materials bought during the same three months of the previous year provide the balance of materials required, and they are charged against current production at their historic costs. The difference between the total value of the materials bought during the last three months of the accounting year and the value, at their original costs, of the same materials purchased during the corresponding three months of the previous year is a revaluation surplus which is included in the profits of the accounting year. Although stocks are turned over every three months so that no single good is deemed to remain in stock more than three months, the revaluation surplus depends on the increase in prices over the entire year. In this very simple example, the revaluation surplus can be approximated by the quantity of stocks held multiplied by the increase in their price from the middle of the previous November to the November of the current accounting year. An alternative way of interpreting the revaluation surplus is to imagine every single input into the process of production as being costed at its price three months previously: from this point of view, the revaluation surplus is equal to the total quantity of inputs consumed during the year multiplied by the average increase in their price over a period of three months.

This simple example illustrates several important points. First, and most obvious, the faster the rate of inflation the greater the revaluation surplus. Second, the longer goods are held in stock, and hence the greater the ratio of stocks to the flow of production, the greater the revaluation surplus. Third, a revaluation surplus does not require any deliberate manipulation of stock levels: fluctuations in stocks complicate the situation, but it is not necessary to engage in speculation in order to record a substantial revaluation surplus.

In national accounts, it is customary to estimate stock appreciation residually. The value of aggregate changes in stocks at current prices is estimated by the approximate method described in the previous section and then this figure is subtracted from the aggregate value of changes in stocks recorded in business accounts at historic costs. This indirect method has to be employed because the values of stock changes which appear in business accounts depend upon the accounting conventions adopted, and these are not uniform, as already mentioned. If, however, all firms used FIFO together with historic costs it would be possible to estimate stock appreciation directly instead of residually, and it is instructive to see how such a direct estimate is related to the indirect one actually in use.

Suppose all firms use FIFO and historic cost accounting and let

q_t = quantity of stocks held at the end of the current accounting period
q_{t-1} = quantity of stocks held at the end of the previous period
p_t = their price at the end of the current period
p_{t-1} = their price at the end of the previous period

Then, the revaluation surplus, or stock appreciation, in respect of a single commodity can be estimated approximately by the formula:

$$R = \overline{q}\,(p_t - p_{t-1}) \tag{1}$$

where $\overline{q}$ is the average level of stocks held throughout the period. It may, in turn, be necessary to approximate $\overline{q}$ by $\frac{1}{2}(q_t + q_{t-1})$ in which case (1) is rewritten as

$$R = \tfrac{1}{2}(q_t + q_{t-1})(p_t - p_{t-1}) \tag{2}$$

In practice, the data available on stocks are more likely to refer to values than quantities, at least at a macro-economic level. In that case, quantities have to be replaced by values deflated by prices or price indices. If v_t is used to denote the value of the stocks held at the end of the current accounting period at the prices then prevailing (i.e., $v_t = p_t q_t$) then equation (2) can be rewritten as follows in the case of a single commodity:

$$R = \tfrac{1}{2}\left(\frac{v_t}{p_t} + \frac{v_{t-1}}{p_{t-1}}\right)(p_t - p_{t-1}) \tag{3}$$

$$= \tfrac{1}{2}\left(v_t \frac{p_{t-1}}{p_t} + v_{t-1}\right)\left(\frac{p_t}{p_{t-1}} - 1\right) \tag{4}$$

The aggregative version of (4) is:

$$R = \tfrac{1}{2}\left(\frac{\Sigma v_t}{\pi} + \Sigma v_{t-1}\right)(\pi - 1) \tag{5}$$

where π is an appropriate price index for the end of the current accounting period based on the end of the previous period (when it equals unity). Equation (5) shows a convenient and practical way in which to approximate the value of total stock appreciation at an aggregative level (assuming FIFO is universally practised).

If stock appreciation is estimated indirectly or residually, the first step is to approximate the value at current prices of the change in stocks, using the approximate method recommended in the SNA and conventionally practised by national accountants:

$$\Delta s = \overline{p}\,(q_t - q_{t-1}) \tag{6}$$

where Δs denotes the change in stocks for a single commodity. Taking the approximation one stage further by replacing $\overline{p}$, the average price over the entire period, by $\frac{1}{2}(p_t + p_{t-1})$, equation (6) becomes

$$\Delta s = \tfrac{1}{2}(p_t + p_{t-1})(q_t - q_{t-1}) \tag{7}$$

$$\text{or } \Delta s = \tfrac{1}{2}\left(\frac{p_t}{p_{t-1}} + 1\right)\left(v_t \frac{p_{t-1}}{p_t} - v_{t-1}\right) \tag{8}$$

which at an aggregative level becomes

$$\Delta s = \tfrac{1}{2}(\pi + 1)\left(\frac{\Sigma v_t}{\pi} - \Sigma v_{t-1}\right) \tag{9}$$

In effect, this is the formula used by national accountants to measure changes in stocks, although it may not be customary to present it in this from.

Under FIFO, the goods remaining in stock are those most recently acquired so that the change in the value of stocks which is recorded between the beginning and end of the accounting period is approximately equal to $\sum v_t - \sum v_{t-1}$. (In practice, the goods held in stock at time t under FIFO will be valued at prices prevailing in the few weeks up to and including time t, but all the formulae under consideration are approximations only). Subtracting Δs as defined in (8) from $\sum v_t - \sum v_{t-1}$, we have:

$$\sum v_t - \sum v_{t-1} - \tfrac{1}{2}(\pi + 1)\left(\frac{\sum v_t}{\pi} - \sum v_{t-1}\right)$$

$$= \tfrac{1}{2}\left(\frac{\sum v_t}{\pi} + \sum v_{t-1}\right)(\pi - 1) = R \qquad (10)$$

Thus, the estimate of stock appreciation obtained residually in national accounts is, in fact, equal to the direct estimate as proposed in equation (5) when FIFO is used. The advantage of (5) is that its meaning is clearer and it is easier to interpret.

It must be reiterated that these results are only approximations and they rest on the assumption of FIFO combined with historic cost accounting. For example, if LIFO were to be used the values of the goods remaining in stock at the end of each accounting period as recorded in business accounts are quite different, and none of the above formulae are applicable. LIFO is examined in a later section.

Equation (5) shows just how large revaluation surpluses can be when prices rise substantially between the beginning and end of the accounting period, but it may be asked whether these are "real" profits or mere "paper" profits generated by the use of arbitrary accounting conventions. The answer has to be the same as for revaluation surpluses generated by stocks of fixed or durable capital goods. The profits are real enough, assuming that FIFO is a proper representation of reality, but their disposal is liable to be prevented, or pre-empted, by simultaneous losses in the purchasing power of the funds used to finance the stock holdings, unless these funds have been borrowed from others. If the firm relies entirely on its own funds it has continually to plough back the whole of the revaluation surpluses received in order to maintain the same level of stocks as before because the funds already invested are no longer adequate for that purpose.

Overall, therefore, the firm is neither better nor worse off, the losses in the real purchasing power of funds already invested counterbalancing the revaluations surpluses on stocks of physical goods. On the other hand, if stocks are purchased entirely out of borrowed funds, no counterbalancing occurs and the enterprise is able to enjoy the surplus without incurring the loss. A net redistribution of real wealth takes place from the lender of the funds to the enterprise which borrows them. The enterprise has continually to increase its borrowing each period to match the price increases in its stocks in order to benefit from this continual redistribution of wealth, a policy which may be neither possible nor desirable in the long run. In between the two extremes of relying entirely on internal or on borrowed funds, there are any number of intermediate possibilities whose implications are fairly clear.

The above discussion has been conducted mainly with reference to average or aggregate profits. However, individual enterprises have considerable scope to increase their own revaluation surpluses if they are successful in anticipating major price increases. While an enterprise may be in the grip of inflationary forces outside its control, it may have more or less success in adapting to those forces. It is not so helpless as in the case of increases in the prices of fixed or durable capital goods which it has already purchased sometime in the past. By accelerating, or decelerating, the rate at which it purchases stocks of non-durable goods it is enabled to engineer for itself revaluation surpluses which deviate considerably from the average for most enterprises. On the other hand, the rate of decline in the purchasing power of funds over designated goods and services is the same whether or not they are actually used for that purpose. Suppose a firm allocates 1 000 units of currency for the purchase of a commodity which doubles in price within the accounting period; at the end of the period the purchasing power of those 1 000 units over the commodity in question, has been halved. If, however, the doubling in price took place suddenly rather than gradually over a long period of time, it does not follow that any revaluation surplus will have been received because the 1 000 units may have been used to purchase the commodity after the price increase occurred. Another enterprise, having correctly foreseen the price rise, may have been successful in borrowing 10 000 units of currency to enlarge its stocks prior to the price increase, in which case it will continue to realise revaluation surpluses over subsequent accounting periods even if there are no further price increases. These examples are intended merely to illustrate that individual enterprises have considerable room to manœuvre in their attempts to mitigate the effects of inflation on their costs of production. As always, averages or aggregates inevitably conceal a great deal of variation and some enterprises may be much more successful than others in coping with inflation, not merely in respect of the extent to which they are able to finance their purchases of goods out of borrowed funds but also in the timing and volume of those purchases.

Finally, it is interesting to note that proposals are under consideration in some countries to introduce an adjustment to the "cost of sales" as shown in business accounts calculated at historic cost, the adjustment being intended to eliminate part or all of the revaluation surplus on stocks. For example, the "Sandilands Report"[1] in the United Kingdom recommended an adjustment which is essentially the same as that practised for many years in national accounts in those countries, such as the UK or USA., which convert profits as reported by businesses onto a basis which is similar to that recommended in the SNA. In business accounts, the "cost of sales" is equal to purchases within the period plus opening stocks minus closing stocks. The intention of the proposal "cost of sales adjustment" is to replace opening stocks minus closing stocks as reported in business accounts by the change in the quantity of stocks between the beginning and end of the year valued at the average prices for the year. The latter is, of course, identical with SNA's approximate estimate of the value of changes in stocks at current prices. The intention appears to be the same as in the SNA, namely to make it possible to obtain an estimate of the value of additions to, and withdrawals from, stock at the prices prevailing when they actually occur. It is suggested that use might be made of special price indices compiled for the inputs typically used by different kinds of industries in order to adjust the prices at which stocks are valued at the beginning and end of the year to average prices for the year. The use of special indices has the advantage that the valuation adjustment is not based on the subjective estimates of individual accountants or managers, but on independent statistics which are the same for whole groups of enterprises. The adjustment can easily be verified by auditors therefore. On the other hand, the average price change for a particular group of commodities, held in stock by an individual enterprise will not be exactly the same as that shown by a general price index, depending on how closely the commodity composition of its stocks matches the commodity weights of the price index. Even if the

1. *Inflation Accounting, Report of the Inflation Accounting Committee,* HMSO (London, Sept. 1975), Cmnd. 6225.

weighting were correct, moreover, the adjustment proposed is still only an approximation, in much the same way that the corresponding procedure recommended in the SNA is recognised to be only an approximation, because it does not take into account any fluctuations in stock levels within the accounting period. Notwithstanding these limitations, the suggested procedure represents a great step forward because it allows gross profits at historic costs to be divided between the gross operating surplus and the revaluation surplus on stocks. The gain in information is considerable during inflation, even if the division is only rough and ready. It must be emphasised, however, that complete accuracy and objectivity are properties to which no system of accounting can lay claim. FIFO itself is only a *convention* which, however plausible or objective it may seem to some people, is still only a working hypothesis. Moreover, valuations of stocks cannot be wholly objective in practice whatever methods are used.

LIFO

Some of the problems described in the previous section may be avoided if the LIFO convention is adopted instead of FIFO. Moreover, LIFO is a permissible form of accounting in several countries and is accepted by tax authorities in those countries. A short summary of the practices adopted in different countries is given in the next section.

As already indicated, the distinction between LIFO and FIFO is quite separate from that between historic and current cost accounting. LIFO, like FIFO, is combined with historic cost accounting, but the goods remaining in stock at the end of the period are deemed to be those first acquired and they are valued accordingly. So long as the physical quantities of stocks are not reduced between the beginning and end of the accounting year, the goods in stock at the end of the year are deemed to include all those there at the start of the year without any change in their value.

No revaluation surpluses on stocks can occur, therefore, so long as stocks are not reduced. The balance sheet valuations of stocks under LIFO may be at prices prevailing many years previously, so that stocks may be grossly undervalued as compared with FIFO.

The implications of LIFO can be illustrated by taking the same simple example as was used for FIFO in which stocks are equal to three months purchases (in the case of inputs) or sales (in the case of outputs). If the level of stocks remains constant and if they consist of homogeneous goods which are physically indistinguishable from each other (raw materials, fuel oil, mass produced items, etc.) no revaluation surpluses are realised as prices rise. By assumption, the goods initially held in stock remain in stock and are neither used nor sold. While there may perhaps be unrealised revaluation surpluses, it can be argued that no realised holding gains have occurred. This, in effect, is the rationale underlying LIFO, and it is not without justification. If stocks are unchanged under LIFO there must be a perfect match over the period as a whole between purchases of materials and intermediate consumption, and also between sales and gross output.

When stocks increase the situation is unchanged in practice. The net additions to stock must be valued at their current prices under LIFO so that no revaluation surpluses are registered.

When stocks are reduced, however, revaluation surpluses are realised under LIFO and they are measured not by the price increases during the accounting period but by the entire cumulative price increase since the goods were first deemed to have been acquired. The birds really come home to roost when this occurs.

The possibility of exceptionally large revaluation surpluses being recorded under what might be difficult conditions for the firm is one of the less attractive features of LIFO. It could be overcome by periodic revaluations of stocks in the balance sheet, although tax authorities might object to such revaluations. When some stocks are increasing and others decreasing, the administration of LIFO may also become complicated although this is no longer so serious an objection as it used to be before the development of electronic business machines.

In the very long run, the only difference between LIFO and FIFO is in the time at which the revaluation surpluses are recorded. If a finite investment project is imagined with definite starting and terminating dates, the total revaluation surpluses using LIFO would be the same as under FIFO although they would be distributed differently over the life of the project. It is likely that the surpluses under LIFO would mostly occur as the project is run down, and certainly at later dates, on average, than those based on FIFO. In real life, the project may never be terminated so that the revaluation surpluses could be deferred indefinitely. Moreover, even if they are eventually realised, there are obvious advantages to a firm in deferring the payment of taxes on them as long as possible; in this respect, there are similarities with accelerated depreciation. Even though the future is uncertain, and tax rates or laws are liable to be changed, the attractions of deferring the payment of tax as long as possible, and conveivably indefinitely, do not need to be laboured.

Although undoubtedly more complicated to administer than FIFO, one advantage claimed for LIFO as a remedy for the problems created by artificially inflated profits during price inflation is that it is easy for accountants to switch over from FIFO to LIFO because no major changes in accounting principles are involved. Even the principle of historic cost accounting can remain inviolate. Thus, many of the advantages of current cost accounting are obtained almost, as it were, by sleight of hand. Even the underlying rationale of LIFO is not altogether unreasonable as a description of processes taking place in the real world, although FIFO appears more plausible in general. Nevertheless, LIFO appears a dubious compromise in which the practical necessity to practise current cost accounting in a world of changing prices is recognised while the principles on which it is based are stubbornly and unreasonably rejected.

Country practices

In this section the accounting conventions used in various countries in 1975 for purposes of valuing stocks are summarized. In general, it may be presumed that FIFO is practised unless stated to the country. The methods summarized are those used to calculate profits *for tax purposes.*

Austria

Stock is usually valued at cost or market value, whichever is the lower. LIFO is permitted, if it can be economically justified.

Belgium

Stock is usually valued at cost or market value, whichever is the lower. LIFO and base stock (current cost) accounting methods are not allowed by law, although no specific system is compulsory.

Denmark

Stock is usually valued at cost or market value, whichever is the lower. For tax purposes, however, the value of stock may be reduced by up to 30 per cent.

France

Stock is valued at cost or market value whichever is the lower.

Germany

Stock is valued at cost or market value, whichever is the lower. Both FIFO and LIFO are allowed; other systems, with the exception of the base stock system, are also permitted if they can be economically justified.

Ireland

Stock is usually valued at cost or market value, whichever is the lower. No regulations are imposed by law.

Italy

Stock is usually valued at cost or market value, whichever is the lower. The use or LIFO is permitted.

Netherlands

Stock is usually valued at cost or market value, whichever is the lower, although other methods may be used. Both FIFO and LIFO are allowed, and also the base stock system. Whatever system is employed must accord with sound commercial practice and be consistently applied.

Norway

Stock is usually valued at cost or market value, whichever is the lower.

Spain

Stock is usually valued at cost or market value, whichever is the lower.

Sweden

Stock may be valued at not less than 40 per cent of the cost or market value, whichever is the lower.

Switzerland

Stock may be valued at not less than two-thirds of the cost or market value, whichever is the lower.

United Kingdom

Stock is usually valued at cost or market value whichever is the lower. LIFO and the base stock system are not permitted. As from November 1974, stocks can be valued at their previous year's values: the system is under review and liable to be changed.

United States

Stock is usually valued at cost or market value whichever is the lower. LIFO is permitted provided it is applied consistently.

(*Principal source:* The International Bureau of Fiscal Documentation.)

There are few countries, therefore, where FIFO and historic cost accounting are rigorously applied without exception. There are two ways in which the distortion of company profits by inflation has been tacitly acknowledged by tax authorities. One concession has been to continue with FIFO and historic cost accounting in principle, but to allow the book value of stocks at the end of the accounting period to be reduced by some arbitrary amount in practice—30 per cent in Denmark, 33 per cent in Switzerland, 60 per cent in Sweden and by a crude estimate of the year's stock appreciation in the United Kingdom. A second concession has been to sanction the use of LIFO, as in Austria, Germany, Italy, the Netherlands, and the United States.

It has been observed in countries such as the United States, in which the use of LIFO has been sanctioned, that by no means all firms are anxious to change over from FIFO to LIFO, despite the immediate tax benefits which LIFO confers during inflation. One reason may be that firms may be worried about the possibility of very large revaluation surpluses occurring in the future if for some reason they have to liquidate all their stocks. It is doubtful, however, whether this possibility is a matter of serious concern to the large business corporation. A more likely explanation for the reluctance to adopt LIFO is an almost instinctive aversion to adopting any procedure which lowers reported profits not merely for tax purposes but to the world at large.

The issues involved are unfamiliar and not generally understood, and a firm may feel that its financial or stock market rating might be jeopardised by a reduction in reported profits when not all firms are experiencing a reduction for the same reason. Whether or not a firm's status would actually be affected is beside the point: what matters is whether management guess that it might be adversely affected. Another factor which might influence a firm's management not to change from FIFO to LIFO is the professionally ingrained conservatism of accountants, for whom the axiom of prudence is easily translated into resistance to change. Finally, management and other employees may conceivably oppose a measure to reduce profits out of self interest if there are incentive schemes which link bonuses to profits. Taking account of all these factors, therefore, it is not surprising there may be some reluctance by individual enterprises to adopt LIFO when there is no compulsion.

Stock appreciation and inflation

To conclude this chapter, the relationship between stock appreciation and inflation is examined empirically. Once again data for the United States and United Kingdom are used for purposes of illustration. No significance is to be read into the choice of these two countries other than that they happen to have data available in a suitable form. In both countries, the profit figures shown in the national accounts are derived from those published in business accounts after various adjustments, the most important of which is for stock appreciation itself. Most other countries do not publish any aggregate figure for stock appreciation because it is not needed when aggregate profits are estimated in a different way.

As already stated, it is quite wrong, therefore, to conclude because no figure is shown for stock appreciation in the national accounts of some country, that stock appreciation is not a major component of gross business profits at historic costs in that country.

In the accompanying table, stock appreciation is shown as a percentage of gross corporate profits for the years 1966 to 1976 inclusive, the estimates for 1976 being provisional. These percentages are compared with the year to year percentage changes in the wholesale price index. It should be noted that the relationship between the two statistics cannot be expected to reflect an underlying structural relationship which is the same for all countries or periods of time. Obviously, the adjustment for stock appreciation must depend on the accounting practices followed in each country, and in particular on the extent to which current cost accounting, or some placebo for it such as LIFO, is used. Nevertheless, for a given country, a close relationship may be expected between the relative size of stock appreciation and the relative movement of wholesale prices, so long as accounting practices remain unchanged.

Such a close relationship can be observed for both countries. In the United States, the two statistics have been approximately equal to each other year by year; in the United Kingdom stock appreciation as a percentage of gross profits has tended to be equal to roughly twice the rate of inflation. The correlations are obviously very strong in both cases. The differences observed between the two countries may be explained by the fact that LIFO is permissible in the United States which would tend to reduce stock appreciation at any given rate of inflation as compared with the United Kingdom where LIFO has been prohibited by the Courts.

1973, when inflation was accelerating rapidly, was an exceptional year for both countries, because stock appreciation was distinctly lower than would be expected from the general relationship which is observed for other years. Were it not for the 1973 figures, the correlations would be almost perfect. Finally, the data in the table illustrate the size of the problem. The sums involved in the years 1973 to 1976 are very considerable by any standards; as mentioned at the beginning of this chapter, they have been known to exceed the amounts paid out in dividends.

Table 5.1 STOCK APPRECIATION AND INFLATION

Year	United States				United Kingdom			
	$ billion				£ million			
	Gross corporate profits[a] (1)	Inventory valuation adjustment (2)	(2) as % of (1) (3)	Annual % change in wholesale price index[b] (4)	Gross trading profits of companies[c] (5)	Stock appreciation (6)	(6) as % of (5) (7)	Annual % change in wholesale price index[d] (8)
1966	114.7	2.1	1.8	1.7	4 610	298	6.5	1.8
1967	114.7	1.7	1.5	0.8	4 663	148	3.2	3.2
1968	126.7	3.4	2.7	2.8	5 275	470	8.9	4.5
1969	129.1	5.5	4.3	4.8	5 314	590	11.1	5.2
1970	122.8	5.1	4.2	2.3	5 669	891	15.7	6.6
1971	138.0	5.0	3.6	3.9	6 585	831	12.6	5.3
1972	156.7	6.6	4.2	6.5	7 656	1 067	13.9	8.4
1973	182.1	18.4	10.1	18.2	9 552	2 546	26.7	27.2
1974	203.2	38.5	18.9	20.9	10 250	4 908	47.9	30.1
1975	209.3	11.4	5.4	4.2	9 961	4 107	41.2	18.0
1976	254.2	14.6	5.7	4.7	12 666	5 182	40.9	21.8

Sources: United States: *Survey of Current Business.* United Kingdom: *Economic Trends.*

a) Gross corporate profits without inventory valuation adjustment.
b) Percentage changes from December to December.
c) Gross trading profits of all non-nationalised companies before providing for stock appreciation.
d) Percentage changes from 4th quarter to 4th quarter: average of the changes for the indices for inputs and outputs.

Chapter 6

PROFIT SHARES AND RATES OF RETURN BY COUNTRY

INTRODUCTION

In this chapter, profit shares and rates of return are presented for a number of countries covering the period 1955 to 1976. The profit shares are defined as the shares of the gross or net operating surplus in gross or net value added, while the rates of return are the ratios of the gross or net operating surplus to the gross or net capital stock. Because the capital stock is measured by cumulating investment backwards, the gross or net rate of return defined in this way is related to the internal rate of return on investment, but in most circumstances seems likely to exceed the latter as explained in Chapters 2 and 3. Operating surpluses must be measured at current costs when they are intended to measure the profits on processes of production carried on within the current accouting period and all the data used in this chapter are compiled at current cost. It is not proposed to present data for the economy as a whole because they would be too heterogenous, and interest is focused instead on corporate and quasi-corporate enterprises engaged in the production of goods and services. For these enterprises, the operating surplus is the appropriate concept of profit. Their long-term viability depends on the efficiency with which their productive operations are carried out, and any revaluation surpluses which they may happen to receive during a period of general inflation are best regarded as windfalls over which they have little control and which may be offset anyway, in whole or in part, by losses in the real value of the funds invested in businesses by their owners.

Sources and coverage of the data

The operating surpluses are taken from national accounts. In principle, they are all consistent with the SNA concept of the operating surplus which has been described at some length in Chapter 4. The details of the statistical sources and publications used are given in the Appendix tc this chapter. The Appendix also lists the sources from which the capital stock data were obtained. There is no standard methodology for compiling capital stock estimates but in practice the perpetual inventory method is generally used whereby capital stock estimates are obtained by cumulating investment data backwards (at constant prices)[1]. Probably rather less confidence can be placed in the comparability between countries in the capital stock estimates than in the estimates of profits. Movements over time within a country, however, should not be very sensitive to any such incomparabilities. The capital stock data do not include either inventories or land: these omissions are important and should be borne in mind in the interpretation and use of the data. The operating surplus includes the return on these two items, whereas they themselves are excluded from the denominators of the rates of return. Their omission may also affect inter-national comparability in so far as these items may be more important for some countries than others.

1. See Michael Ward, *op. cit.*

Data are presented for two groups of enterprises, namely manufacturing and all industry plus transport and communications. The choice of the latter group requires some explanation. In principle, it was intended to compile data for all non-financial corporate and quasi-corporate enterprises, and the group industry plus transport and communications is used as a proxy for it. The rationale behind this particular choice is as follows. First, all unincorporated enterprises should be excluded as far as possible. It is impossible to break down the income received by owners of unincorporated enterprises into its wage and profit elements without the use of quite arbitrary assumptions. Even if it could be done, however, the distinction between wages and profits would not have the same significance as in corporate or quasi-corporate enterprises because there is not the same conflict of interest when both incomes are received by the same person. As it is not possible to separate both the income and capital stock data for unincorporated enterprises from those for corporate and quasi-corporate enterprises, it was decided, as a second best solution, to eliminate those industries in which unincorporated enterprises predominate. This is feasible because both income and capital stock can be broken down by industry. The industries excluded on this criterion were agriculture, distribution and miscellaneous services. The exclusion of agriculture has the added advantage that it reduces the significance of the exclusion of land from the capital stock figures.

The services of general government were excluded on the grounds that the net operating surplus is deemed by convention to be zero for these activities. It is also desirable to exclude the capital owned by the government because no output is attributed to much of it, e.g. roads. Income from the ownership of dwellings was excluded because it has no wage element, and all residential dwellings are correspondingly excluded from the capital stock figures. Finally, financial intermediaries—banks, insurance, etc.—were excluded because their principle activity is not the production of goods and services destined for sale: the operating surplus is not very relevant to these enterprises.

By a process of elimination, therefore, the coverage is reduced to the following five industry groups:

Mining	Public utilities
Manufacturing	Transport and communications
Construction	

The first four are the industries normally covered by an index of industrial production, and it was decided to call the group of five "all industry plus transport". Because of its intrinsic importance it was also decided to compile data for manufacturing on its own when it became clear that it is possible to obtain the necessary data.

As stated above, the group "industry plus transport" is intended to be a proxy for all corporate and quasi-corporate enterprises. Given that the statistics presented here are all *ratios* of one variable to another, the fact that the coverage is not exactly that desired does not necessarily introduce any bias. Unfortunately, because of the limited breakdown of the capital stock figures available for the United States, the data presented for the USA have to be for a broader group of industries than "industry plus transport": they also include distribution and miscellaneous services.

The Data

The basic data are presented in Tables 6.1 to 6.4. These tables show profit shares and rates of return both gross and net and also for both manufacturing and all industry plus transport. The countries covered are all those for which it has been possible to obtain the requisite data on the operating surplus even though in three cases the corresponding capital stock figures are not available. The period covered is from 1955 to the latest year with data available, which is usually either 1975 or 1976.

There are three variables involved for which the following symbols are used in the tables:

P = Operating surplus, gross or net
Y = Value added, gross or net
K = Capital stock, gross or net

It is always clear in context whether the variables are defined gross or net. Gross and net variables are never mixed together, all ratios being either gross/gross or net/net. There are, of course, three ratios which can be calculated and they are inter-related as follows:

$$\frac{P}{K} \equiv \frac{P}{Y} \cdot \frac{Y}{K} \qquad (6.1)$$

In words, the rate of return on capital is identical with the share of the operating surplus in value added multiplied by the ratio of value added to the capital stock. The last of the three ratios is the reciprocal of the familiar capital/output ratio, and it will be referred to as "capital productivity". It is implied by the other two ratios and it was decided to show it explicitly in the tables alongside them.

Although 6.1 is an identity it can be useful in interpreting the data. If, for example, the rate of return for a particular period or country is relatively high it can be determined to what extent this is due to a relatively high share of profits or to a relatively high capital productivity. It is useful to be able to distinguish in this way, even if only superficially, the effects of the distribution of factor incomes on the rate of return on capital from those of the efficiency with which capital is utilised in production.

There are three countries, Australia, Denmark and the Netherlands, for which it has been possible to obtain some data on factor income shares for the relevant industries, but not the corresponding capital stock figures. These income shares are shown in the final three rows of Tables 6.1 to 6.4. There are a few other countries for which the distribution of factor income is available for the economy as a whole but not sub-divided by industry; these are not shown on grounds of lack of comparability.

The data given in Tables 6.1 to 6.4 on profit shares and rates of return are shown graphically in Diagram 6.1 to 6.4. It is not proposed to comment on the individual figures given in the tables and graphs but to try to condense this information by means of summary statistics obtained by fitting trends to the observations. This is the subject of the next and final section.

Trends in factor shares and rates of return

In order to make it possible to assimilate the mass of detailed information given in Tables 6.1 to 6.4, time trends have been fitted to all the series and the results are presented in Tables 6.5 and 6.6.

The functional form chosen is that of the exponential time trend, or semi-logarithmic trend as it is often called. In the case of the factor shares, for example, the trend fitted is as follows:

$$P/Y = ae^{bt} \qquad (6.2)$$

or

$$\log_e \left(\frac{P}{Y}\right) = \log_e a + bt \qquad (6.3)$$

Estimates of a and b have been obtained by using ordinary least-squares on equation 6.3. The resulting estimates are given in Tables 6.5 and 6.6 under the headings of "trend level" and "rate of change" respectively. The values of b have been multiplied by 100 so that they actually show the percentage rates of change per year. These should not be confused with the number of points by which a percentage share or ratio changes per year. For example, if the level of some share is 20 per cent, and its percentage rate of decline as given by 100b is 5 per cent per year, this means that it falls from 20 to 19 (i.e. by $20 \times \frac{5}{100}$) and not from 20 to 15.

There are two reasons for choosing the particular functional form used, despite the tiresome ambiguity in percentage rates of change in percentages just referred to. The first, and less important, is that this type of function precludes negative values and postulates that the absolute rate of decline of a share, or ratio, slows down the smaller the share becomes. While this may be reasonable for trend values it should be noticed that operating surpluses, especially the net surplus, can in fact be negative in individual periods.

The second and more important reason is that the use of the semi-logarithmic time trend preserves in the estimated coefficients the relationship embodied in equation 6.1.
Obviously,

$$\log \left(\frac{P}{K}\right) \equiv \log \left(\frac{P}{Y}\right) + \log \left(\frac{Y}{K}\right) \qquad (6.4.)$$

If each of these three variables in log form is regressed on the same variable, namely time, the resulting coefficients for $\log \left(\frac{P}{Y}\right)$ and $\log \left(\frac{Y}{K}\right)$ sum identically to those for $\log \left(\frac{P}{K}\right)$. As a result, the time trends for the rates of return $\frac{P}{K}$ shown in Tables 6.5 and 6.6, can be decomposed into two components denoting the time trends to the profits shares $\frac{P}{Y}$ and in the capital productivities $\frac{Y}{K}$ respectively. For example, the 1.80 rate of decline in $\frac{P}{K}$ for Canada in the first row of Table 6.5 can be split into two components, one of which is a rate of decline of 0.63 per cent in $\frac{P}{Y}$ and the other is a decline of 1.17 per cent in $\frac{Y}{K}$.

The constant terms in the regression are also additive in logarithmic form, but these have to be anti-logged to get them into a meaningful form, as can be seen from equations 6.2 and 6.3 above. In consequence, the levels shown in Tables 6.5 and 6.6 are multiplicative rather than additive. For example, working with pure numbers rather than percentages, the figure of 0.132 for $\frac{P}{K}$ for Canada in the first row of Table 6.5 is identical with $\frac{P}{Y} \cdot \frac{Y}{K}$ or 0.317×0.414. This relationship is particularly useful when comparing levels between countries. For example, the gross rate of return in Canada just noted is much lower than that in the United States, 0.219, shown in the line immediately below it in Table 6.5. However, it can be seen that this is entirely due to a much lower capital productivity in Canada, because the share of the gross operating surplus in gross value added is actually higher in Canada in the United States.

One final point should be noted about the levels shown in Tables 6.5 and 6.6. Once a trend is fitted to a set of data it is purely a matter of convenience which year is chosen to exhibit the level of the expected values. Usually, the first year is chosen but the last year has been chosen here as there is obviously more interest in recent trend values than in more remote ones. The trend levels given in Tables 6.5 and 6.6 can be interpreted in much the same way as average figures because they depend upon the values of the entire series of observations. More formally, they are the values of a in equations 6.2 and 6.3 which are obtained by choosing the last year as the time origin—that is by fixing $t=0$ in the last year covered.

Because of serial correlation in the residuals about the fitted trends it is not possible to establish proper significance levels for the estimates. Nevertheless, it is useful to be able to distinguish *comparative* levels of significance even if the absolute probabilities cannot be determined. Accordingly, a single asterisk is attached to a rate of change for which the t statistic is greater than 3, while a double asterisk signifies t greater than 5.

Trends have been fitted for two overlapping time periods. Profit shares and rates of return were relatively low in the mid 1970's in most countries, so that time trends which end in 1975 or 1976 are likely to be unduly influenced by the data for the last two or three years. To reduce the risk of bias two alternative procedures have been adopted. The first is simply to omit data for 1974 onwards and to fit time trends covering the years 1955 to 1973. The resulting trends are given in the upper halves of Tables 6.5 and 6.6. The second is to retain the years after 1973 but to start the series in the first year covered in which profit shares and rates of return were at a cyclical low. As can be seen from Diagrams 6.1 to 6.4 the appropriate starting year is 1958, so that time trends have also been fitted for the period 1958 to 1976, and these are given in the lower halves of Tables 6.5 and 6.6.

The following points may be made about the general interpretation of the figures in Tables 6.5 and 6.6 and the original data in Tables 6.1 to 6.4 on which they are based. First, more confidence may be placed in movements over time than in the absolute levels of the various ratios or shares. Second, the income data are probably more comparable between countries than the capital stock data, so that comparisons of profit shares are probably more reliable than comparisons of rates of return. Third, the decomposition of rates of return into profit shares and capital productivities is merely an identity which does not throw any light on directions of causality. In particular, the rate of return should not be treated as the dependent variable and the other two as independent when all three may be determined simultaneously.

In the interests of orderly presentation a system of sub-headings will be used below because of the large number of relationships involved.

Manufacturing

Manufacturing: rates of return

a) Levels

Trend rates of return at the end of both periods, whether measured gross or net, were highest in Japan and the United States and lowest in the United Kingdom, Sweden and Italy. The differences between the two extremes were quite considerable, the highest rates of return being three, four or even five times higher than the lowest.

b) Rates of change

Rates of return have been subject to significant fluctuations in both Japan and the United States which make the identification of long term trends difficult. There is no clear evidence of a long term decline for either country, and it is noticeable that rates of return made a strong recovery between 1974 and 1976 in the United States. This confirms the results of some other recent investigations which suggest that it is premature to conclude that there is a downward trend in rates of return in US manufacturing. While the data for Japan ending in 1976 suggest a downward trend, the data for 1955 to 1973 do not.

On the other hand, the data for the European OECD countries covered consistently display downward trends. The decline is least marked for Sweden, but this was partly because rates of return were already at relatively low levels in Sweden even two decades ago. The evidence is clearest for Germany and the United Kingdom where there is no mistaking the downward trends over the whole period.

Manufacturing: profit shares

a) Levels

Profit shares whether gross or net, are highest in Japan. Despite the high rates of return just noted, profit shares are not high in the United States: on the contrary they are comparatively low. The lowest profit shares, however, are those in the United Kingdom, especially the trend figures for 1976.

b) Rates of change

The general situation is similar to that summarised above for rates of return. There is no clear evidence of falling profit shares for Japan and the United States, and also Australia, but the European countries are all fairly consistent in showing declining profit shares. Moreover, these data cover two additional countries, Denmark and the Netherlands, for which no data on capital stock, and hence rates of return, are available.

Manufacturing: capital productivities

a) Levels

Capital productivity is considerably higher in the United States than in any other country, especially the ratio of net value added to net capital. Indeed, net capital productivity is so much higher as to raise some doubts as to whether it is fully comparable statistically with the figures for other countries. A contributory factor may be that the prices of capital goods appear to be relatively low in the United States so that using relative prices of other countries capital productivity might not appear so high as at US prices. Another factor affecting net productivity might be that the depreciation method used to estimate the net capital stock is more accelerated than in other countries. It is certainly not being suggested, however, that the explanation is all statistical and that capital productivity is not high in the United States.

Apart from the United States, the differences between countries are not so great as for rates of return or profit shares. Japan, Germany and Canada have relatively high productivities, and Italy, the United Kingdom and Sweden relatively low figures.

b) Rates of change

The general picture is even less clear than for rates of return and profit shares. While the data for the United Kingdom, Germany, Canada and Sweden suggest declining capital productivities, the evidence for the United States, Japan and Italy is inconclusive.

Manufacturing: country summary

The high rates of return observed for Japan and the United States cannot be explained in the same way. In the case of Japan it reflects a high share of profits in value added, whether measured gross or net, whereas the share of profits in the United States is not high in comparison with European countries the high rate of return reflecting an unusually high capital productivity. While there is some evidence that rates of return may have been falling recently in Japan, the evidence is inconclusive, and it is certainly not possible to discern any long term trend in the US figures.

Rates of return are generally lower in the European countries covered, and they have mostly shown persistent downward trends, which are particularly marked for Germany and the United Kingdom. In the middle and late 1950's rates of return in Germany, whether measured gross or net, were similar on average to those in Japan and the United States, but by the late 1970's they had fallen significantly below them. Rates of return in Italy, Sweden and the United Kingdom have tended to be comparatively low throughout, with the UK rates falling to exceptionally low levels in 1974 to 1976.

Declining rates of return in Europe have been fairly consistently associated with falling shares of profits in value added. The decline in profit shares and rates of return tends to be more pronounced when measured net rather than gross because capital consumption has tended to increase its share of gross value added in all countries, a phenomenon which is not shown explicitly in the tables. In Germany the share of net profits in net value added fell from 37 per cent to 16 per cent between 1955 and 1976 while in the United Kingdom it fell from 30 per cent to 7 per cent. In the United Kingdom the severity of the collapse in real rates of return from 9.3 per cent to 2.9 per cent between 1972 and 1975 which was associated with a fall from 19 per cent to 7 per cent in the share of net profits in net value added, was not, and may still not be, perceived by many observers who continue to take historic cost figures seriously during a period of unprecently high rates of inflation[2]. Declining rates of return in Europe are not entirely attributable to falling profit shares, however, as there has also been some tendency for capital productivity to fall in most countries as can be seen from the coefficients in Table 6.5.

Industry plus transport

All industry plus transport: rates of return

a) Levels

The group "industry plus transport" is intended as a proxy for all non-financial corporate and quasi-corporate enterprises, as already explained. Rates

2. In an article on rates of return published in the UK *Trade and Industry*, 16th September 1977, it is shown that the net rate of return at *historic* cost based on the published accounts for large listed manufacturing companies in the UK actually rose fractionally from 15.0 per cent in 1972 to 15.5 per cent in 1975. In the same article, it is estimated by the Department of Trade and Industry that at *current* costs the real net rate of return for exactly the same group of companies fell from 8.9 per cent to 2.6 per cent between 1972 and 1975 (Table 2, p. 520).

of return whether measured gross or net tend to be lower than for manufacturing (except in Italy). They are highest in Japan, followed by Germany, the United States and Italy. Unfortunately, the data for the United States include distribution and miscellaneous services and are to that extent less comparable with the figures for other countries. The lowest rates are found in Sweden and the United Kingdom whose data are very similar in many respects.

b) Rates of change

The only country which does not exhibit a systematic tendency for rates of return to decline is Japan. Although rates of return did fall in the early and mid seventies in Japan, they did not fall below the levels of the late fifties, and once again its is difficult to disentangle cycle from trend. Otherwise, each country displays a small but persistent tendency for rates of return, both gross and net, to fall over the longer term. The rate of decline is generally slower than for manufacturing except in Sweden and, of course, the United States where there is no downward trend for manufacturing. The downward trend is also rather more pronounced for the European countries covered, Germany, Italy, Sweden and the United Kingdom, than for Canada and the United States (and, of course, Japan).

Industry plus transport: profit shares

a) Levels

Profit shares, both gross and net, are highest in Japan, Denmark and Germany and lowest in the United Kingdom, Sweden and the United States. The intermediate group of countries consists of Canada, Australia, Italy and the Netherlands.

b) Rates of change

There are few generalisations which apply to every one of this larger group of countries. First, there is no consistent evidence of any significant tendency for profit shares to decline in the case of four countries, Canada, Japan, Australia and Denmark. On the other hand, the evidence is clearly there the United States and the remaining European countries. In general, the rates of decline are slower than for manufacturing. They are also slower for the gross profit shares than for the net shares because capital consumption tends to increase its share of gross value added over time in all countries.

Industry plus transport: capital productivities

a) Levels

The differences between countries are less pronounced than for manufacturing, at least between the extremes. Trend values for gross capital productivities are highest in the United States and Japan and lowest in Canada, Sweden and the United Kingdom, but the ratio from one extreme to the other is less than two to one. The pattern is somewhat different for the net figures where the United States once again emerges on its own as having a very high capital productivity, although the figure is not nearly so exceptional as the corresponding one for manufacturing.

b) Rates of change

For the period ending in 1973, Japan and Italy have upward trends in their capital productivities, while the United States has no trend. Other countries have downward trends over both periods covered.

Industry and transport: country summary

The general picture is roughly similar to manufacturing but with the shades softened and contrasts reduced. The relatively high rates of return observed in Japan, the United States, Germany and Italy are all associated with relatively high capital productivities: these are re-inforced in the case of Japan and Germany by high profit shares but not in the case of the United States and Italy where profit shares are, if anything, on the low side.

Rates of return have been tending to fall slightly in all the countries with data available except Japan where the relatively low rates of return in the seventies are no lower than twenty years previously. Falling rates of return have tended to be associated with both falling profit shares and falling capital productivities, and it is not legitimate to single out one factor rather the other as contributing the more. There is not nearly such strong evidence of declining profit shares as in the case of manufacturing on its own. For example, whereas already noted in manufacturing the shares of net profits in value added fell from 37 per cent to 17 per cent for Germany and from 30 per cent to 7 per cent for the United Kingdom between 1955 and 1976, the corresponding figures for all industry plus transport were 43 per cent falling to 35 per cent for Germany and 24 per cent falling to 14 per cent for the United Kingdom.

Finally, in the case of the three countries with data available on profit shares but not on capital stocks or rates of return, it would appear from the behaviour of their profit shares that Denmark and especially Australia would not display significant or persistent downward trends in rates of return. On the other hand, profit shares in the Netherlands behave similarly to those in Germany and it seems reasonable to infer that there has been a long term decline in rates of return in the Netherlands also.

POSTSCRIPT

The above paragraphs have attempted to summarise various trends in profit shares and rates of return over the two decades from the mid 1950's to the mid 1970's. On balance, the data clearly support the view that profit shares and rates of return have fallen significantly in some countries and certain industries. Moreover, there is next to no evidence anywhere pointing in the opposite direction of increasing profitablity. However, it is appropriate to end by sounding several notes of caution to avoid over-generalising these results. The first is that the two largest OECD countries, the United States and Japan, are precisely the countries where the evidence is least convincing and for which no firm conclusions can be established about the existence of downward trends. The second is that the number of countries studied is fairly small and it is risky to generalise from the experience of only seven countries. A third reason for caution is the difficulty of separating cyclical from trend factors, especially when the run of data ends in a recession. Finally, even when downward trends can be clearly observed, they refer to the past and there is no justification for assuming that the trends will continue outside the range of observations covered. The results show that profits and rates of return have fallen significantly in certain countries, but that is not to say that they are still falling or will continue to fall in the future.

TABLE 6.1 GROSS PROFITS AND RATES OF RETURN: MANUFACTURING

		1955	1956	1957	1958	1959	1960	1961	1962	1963	1964	1965	1966	1967	1968	1969	1970	1971	1972	1973	1974	1975	1976
Canada	P/Y	35.6	36.4	34.5	34.0	34.2	33.4	33.7	35.0	35.6	36.4	34.4	33.1	31.2	32.3	32.0	30.2	31.2	32.3	34.0	34.8	33.3	31.2
	Y/K	54.4	55.0	51.4	47.4	48.0	45.9	44.2	45.6	46.1	46.7	44.8	44.1	43.3	45.0	44.8	41.5	41.0	42.7	45.2	44.5	40.6	40.6
	P/K	19.3	20.0	17.8	16.1	16.4	15.3	14.9	16.0	16.4	17.0	15.4	14.6	13.5	14.6	14.4	12.5	12.8	13.8	15.3	15.5	13.5	12.7
United States	P/Y	28.0	26.0	25.4	23.6	26.1	27.0	26.6	26.8	27.5	28.0	29.5	29.1	27.6	27.5	25.6	23.5	25.0	26.1	25.6	23.8	27.0	28.6
	Y/K	86.3	82.0	78.0	70.0	78.2	80.5	78.5	83.3	85.2	88.1	92.0	94.5	89.0	89.2	85.6	76.5	74.4	78.0	80.7	76.1	71.9	76.8
	P/K	24.1	21.3	19.8	16.5	20.4	21.7	20.9	22.4	23.4	24.7	27.1	27.5	24.5	24.6	21.9	18.0	18.6	20.4	20.7	18.1	19.4	22.0
Japan	P/Y	43.9	43.4	49.2	47.1	47.1	51.8	52.1	49.7	49.3	49.8	47.6	48.0	49.7	50.8	50.8	50.4	47.8	45.6	42.5	39.5	40.3	
	Y/K	45.4	48.9	53.2	51.6	55.0	63.4	63.2	58.9	58.5	58.7	54.7	55.5	59.5	62.3	61.8	61.4	57.7	55.1	52.8	45.6	45.2	
	P/K	19.9	21.2	26.2	24.3	25.9	32.8	32.9	29.2	28.9	29.2	26.0	26.6	29.6	31.7	31.4	30.9	27.6	25.1	22.4	18.0	18.2	
Germany	P/Y	41.1	39.6	39.3	39.5	39.7	38.4	36.7	34.2	33.8	35.2	35.8	33.4	34.9	36.8	35.1	32.5	30.8	28.6	27.1	27.2	25.5	26.4
	Y/K	58.4	57.6	56.3	55.3	55.8	56.9	55.7	53.6	50.7	52.2	52.9	50.9	48.6	52.6	53.6	52.7	50.0	48.7	50.0	49.3	46.0	47.9
	P/K	24.0	22.8	22.1	21.8	22.1	21.9	20.5	18.3	17.1	18.4	19.0	17.0	16.9	19.3	18.8	17.1	15.4	13.9	13.6	13.4	11.7	12.7
Italy	P/Y	41.3	40.4	40.4	39.9	41.2	40.8	40.0	36.8	32.4	29.9	33.5	35.8	33.9	34.5	34.1	31.6	28.8	29.3	29.4	28.2	21.1	
	Y/K	31.0	29.9	28.5	27.4	28.1	29.3	29.8	30.0	29.8	28.0	27.1	28.5	30.2	29.7	30.8	32.3	30.6	30.8				
	P/K	12.8	12.1	11.5	10.9	11.6	12.0	11.9	11.0	9.7	8.4	9.1	10.2	10.2	10.3	10.5	10.2	8.8	9.0				
Sweden	P/Y	31.3	31.9	32.7	32.0	33.9	32.5	30.5	28.9	27.3	29.4	29.9	28.1	28.1	28.9	30.1	33.0	28.4	28.0	34.1	38.4	30.8	25.6
	Y/K	40.6	39.7	40.1	39.9	39.5	39.6	39.2	39.2	36.9	38.1	38.6	37.4	36.9	37.4	38.1	39.9	36.2	35.4	35.7	38.2	37.2	35.9
	P/K	12.7	12.7	13.1	12.7	13.4	12.9	12.0	11.3	10.1	11.2	11.6	10.5	10.4	10.8	11.5	13.2	10.3	9.9	12.1	14.7	11.4	9.2
United Kingdom	P/Y	33.7	32.0	31.9	31.8	32.3	32.9	30.1	29.0	30.6	31.0	30.1	28.0	28.5	28.4	27.6	24.6	25.0	25.8	22.9	18.9	16.0	16.7
	Y/K	40.3	39.2	38.8	38.3	39.6	41.7	40.2	38.2	37.9	39.1	39.2	37.9	36.4	36.6	36.5	35.8	34.6	33.3	32.3	29.6	28.3	26.5
	P/K	13.6	12.5	12.4	12.2	12.8	13.7	12.1	11.1	11.6	12.1	11.8	10.6	10.4	10.4	10.1	8.8	8.6	8.6	7.4	5.6	4.5	4.4
Australia	P/Y	25.9	25.8	27.5	30.4	30.9	29.1	27.6	28.0	34.9	35.2	34.4	33.8	33.5	33.9	34.6	33.4	31.6	29.5	31.0	28.0	22.5	
Denmark	P/Y	42.1	41.5	42.9	43.4	45.8	47.4	46.1	46.3	44.5	45.0	43.7	41.7	41.5	41.8	41.1	40.0	40.0	40.3	39.1	34.2	34.4	
Netherlands	P/Y	45.8	43.5	42.5	40.3	43.3	44.2	40.4	38.8	36.5	37.1	36.8	35.1	34.8	34.8	36.4	35.8	34.3	35.7	34.9	35.7	35.8	

P = Gross operating surplus. Y = Gross value added. K = Gross capital stock.

TABLE 6.2 NET PROFITS AND RATES OF RETURN: MANUFACTURING

		1955	1956	1957	1958	1959	1960	1961	1962	1963	1964	1965	1966	1967	1968	1969	1970	1971	1972	1973	1974	1975	1976
Canada	P/Y	30.8	31.7	29.2	28.1	28.3	27.2	27.2	28.9	29.6	30.4	27.9	26.3	24.2	25.7	25.3	22.7	23.7	25.3	27.6	28.3	25.9	23.7
	Y/K	82.1	82.3	75.3	68.6	69.9	67.2	65.1	67.9	68.8	69.7	66.4	64.8	63.2	66.3	66.4	60.9	60.1	63.2	67.5	66.3	59.8	59.7
	P/K	25.3	26.1	22.0	19.2	19.8	18.2	17.7	19.6	20.3	21.2	18.5	17.0	15.3	17.0	16.8	13.8	14.3	16.0	18.6	18.7	15.5	14.1
United States	P/Y	23.2	20.7	19.6	17.0	20.4	21.5	20.9	21.5	22.3	23.0	24.8	24.5	22.5	22.5	20.2	17.1	18.6	20.1	19.8	17.4	20.4	22.8
	Y/K	148.1	140.2	132.1	117.9	134.8	140.6	138.3	148.8	153.3	159.1	164.8	166.4	153.1	152.1	144.9	128.7	125.8	133.7	139.3	127.3	124.3	135.1
	P/K	34.3	29.0	25.9	20.0	27.5	30.3	29.0	32.0	34.2	36.6	40.9	40.8	34.4	34.2	29.2	22.0	23.4	26.9	27.6	22.2	25.4	30.8
Japan	P/Y	36.6	36.4	42.9	39.7	39.1	44.7	44.0	40.7	40.0	39.7	37.0	37.7	40.3	41.9	41.3	40.9	37.7	35.4	31.8	28.2	29.5	
	Y/K	56.9	61.7	67.2	64.2	67.8	78.4	76.9	71.1	70.4	69.5	64.8	65.9	71.4	75.2	73.9	68.7	62.3	57.2	49.3	46.4	47.2	
	P/K	20.9	22.4	28.8	25.5	26.5	35.0	33.8	28.9	28.2	27.6	23.9	24.9	28.8	31.5	30.6	28.1	23.5	20.2	15.7	13.1	13.9	
Germany	P/Y	36.8	35.0	34.5	34.5	34.7	33.3	31.3	28.1	27.0	28.5	28.9	25.8	26.9	29.6	27.9	24.8	22.5	19.8	18.3	18.1	15.2	16.5
	Y/K	84.5	81.3	78.0	75.8	76.2	77.2	74.8	71.3	67.1	69.4	70.5	67.8	65.1	72.0	74.4	73.2	69.3	67.7	70.4	70.0	65.6	69.5
	P/K	31.1	28.5	26.9	26.2	26.5	25.7	23.4	20.0	18.2	19.8	20.4	17.5	17.5	21.3	20.7	18.2	15.6	13.4	12.9	12.7	10.0	11.4
Italy	P/Y	30.9	30.0	29.9	29.5	31.4	31.6	30.7	27.5	22.6	19.5	23.1	26.2	24.4	25.2	25.1	22.5	19.4	20.1				
	Y/K	46.9	45.6	43.4	42.6	44.2	46.4	46.6	46.3	45.5	42.8	42.0	44.5	47.3	46.7	48.6	51.1	48.6	48.9				
	P/K	14.5	13.7	13.0	12.6	13.9	14.7	14.3	12.7	10.3	8.3	9.7	11.7	11.6	11.8	12.2	11.5	9.4	9.9				
Sweden	P/Y	25.0	25.5	26.4	25.6	27.7	26.2	23.9	22.1	19.9	22.5	23.1	20.8	20.6	21.6	23.4	26.8	21.0	20.4	27.4	32.4	23.3	17.0
	Y/K	55.5	54.2	54.8	54.5	54.0	54.1	53.5	53.4	50.0	51.8	52.6	50.8	49.9	50.7	52.0	54.6	49.0	47.8	48.4	52.1	50.1	48.1
	P/K	13.9	13.8	14.5	13.9	14.9	14.2	12.8	11.8	9.9	11.7	12.2	10.6	10.3	10.9	12.2	14.6	10.3	9.8	13.3	16.9	11.7	8.2
United Kingdom	P/Y	29.6	27.5	27.3	27.0	27.6	28.5	25.2	23.8	25.4	26.0	24.9	22.5	22.8	22.7	21.8	18.4	18.5	19.3	16.1	11.1	7.1	7.3
	Y/K	66.2	63.3	61.4	59.4	60.7	63.6	60.4	56.5	55.8	57.8	57.9	55.8	53.5	53.7	53.5	52.2	50.3	48.5	47.1	43.1	41.1	38.6
	P/K	19.6	17.4	16.7	16.0	16.8	18.1	15.2	13.4	14.1	15.0	14.4	12.5	12.2	12.2	11.6	9.6	9.3	9.3	7.6	4.8	2.9	2.8
Australia	P/Y	22.4	22.0	23.3	25.0	25.4	23.6	21.5	21.4	29.0	29.1	28.1	27.0	26.5	26.9	27.7	26.6	24.8	22.3	24.6	21.9	16.2	
Netherlands	P/Y	40.4	37.9	36.8	34.4	37.7	38.7	34.5	32.8	30.3	30.9	30.5	28.7	28.3	28.3	30.1	29.4	27.8	29.3	28.4	29.4	29.5	33.6

P = Net operating surplus. Y = Net value added. K = Net capital stock.

TABLE 6.3 GROSS PROFITS AND RATES OF RETURN: INDUSTRY PLUS TRANSPORT

		1955	1956	1957	1958	1959	1960	1961	1962	1963	1964	1965	1966	1967	1968	1969	1970	1971	1972	1973	1974	1975	1976
Canada	P/Y	38.0	38.4	36.7	36.3	36.8	36.4	37.0	37.7	38.5	39.4	38.0	37.1	35.8	36.6	36.1	35.2	35.0	36.1	37.9	38.2	36.4	36.1
	Y/K	33.3	33.8	32.0	29.4	29.5	28.5	27.9	28.1	28.4	29.1	29.0	29.2	28.7	29.1	28.7	27.3	26.8	26.9	28.6	28.2	26.0	25.9
	P/K	12.6	13.0	11.7	10.7	10.8	10.3	10.3	10.6	10.9	11.5	11.0	10.8	10.3	10.7	10.4	9.6	9.4	9.7	10.8	10.8	9.5	9.4
United States	P/Y	35.3	34.1	33.9	33.5	34.4	33.8	33.8	33.6	33.8	34.2	34.6	34.2	33.4	33.1	31.8	30.6	31.2	31.3	30.7	29.8	31.6	32.0
	Y/K	55.7	54.0	51.9	48.1	51.4	51.4	50.7	52.5	53.4	55.1	56.4	57.4	55.3	55.3	53.7	49.9	48.7	49.4	50.2	48.0	45.7	47.6
	P/K	19.7	18.4	17.6	16.1	17.7	17.4	17.1	17.7	18.0	18.8	19.5	19.6	18.5	18.3	17.1	15.2	15.2	15.5	15.4	14.3	14.4	15.2
Japan	P/Y	41.2	42.3	45.9	43.6	43.8	47.9	48.9	46.7	46.8	46.6	44.3	44.7	46.2	47.8	48.1	48.1	45.5	44.3	41.4	37.4	37.8	
	Y/K	31.7	33.2	35.3	35.7	38.0	42.6	44.4	43.9	44.8	46.0	43.9	44.5	46.5	48.9	49.2	49.9	48.5	47.5	45.1	38.4	39.8	
	P/K	13.1	14.0	16.2	15.6	16.6	20.4	21.7	20.5	20.9	21.5	19.4	19.9	21.5	23.3	23.7	24.0	22.0	21.1	18.7	14.4	15.1	
Germany	P/Y	47.2	46.7	46.9	46.3	47.1	46.8	45.0	43.8	43.2	43.1	43.5	42.9	43.9	44.9	43.7	42.5	41.9	41.6	40.5	40.2	40.6	41.7
	Y/K	51.4	51.5	51.8	51.7	53.3	54.7	53.1	51.3	48.8	48.5	49.1	47.8	45.3	47.6	47.3	47.6	46.2	45.6	45.8	44.7	42.5	44.0
	P/K	24.3	24.1	24.3	23.9	25.1	25.6	23.9	22.5	21.1	20.9	21.4	20.5	19.9	21.4	20.7	20.2	19.4	19.0	18.6	18.0	17.2	18.4
Italy	P/Y	46.0	45.3	45.8	45.8	46.8	45.8	45.1	42.7	38.6	37.5	40.5	41.7	39.8	40.7	40.9	36.5	33.2	33.6	33.2	33.1	26.9	
	Y/K	37.4	36.9	35.8	35.6	36.8	38.4	39.6	40.4	40.5	39.0	37.7	39.0	40.8	39.7	41.2	41.7	38.5	38.2				
	P/K	17.2	16.7	16.4	16.3	17.2	17.6	17.9	17.3	15.6	14.6	15.3	16.2	16.2	16.2	16.9	15.2	12.8	12.9				
Sweden	P/Y	34.5	35.3	35.7	35.5	36.6	35.2	34.3	32.5	31.3	32.4	33.1	31.2	31.1	31.5	32.2	32.6	28.6	29.1	32.9	34.0	27.4	22.4
	Y/K	31.4	30.8	30.9	30.7	30.1	30.0	29.7	29.7	28.5	29.3	30.0	29.3	29.2	29.4	29.8	29.8	27.0	26.6	25.9	26.1	25.8	25.1
	P/K	10.8	10.9	11.0	10.9	11.0	10.5	10.2	9.6	8.9	9.5	9.9	9.2	9.1	9.3	9.6	9.7	7.7	7.8	8.5	8.9	7.1	5.6
United Kingdom	P/Y	30.7	29.8	29.4	29.2	30.1	31.7	29.7	28.8	30.5	31.0	30.3	29.1	29.7	30.8	30.9	28.6	28.9	30.1	30.7	27.5	24.7	26.7
	Y/K	28.9	28.9	28.8	28.3	29.1	30.9	30.4	29.7	29.8	30.7	30.8	29.9	28.8	29.0	28.6	27.9	27.1	26.7	26.4	24.6	24.1	23.0
	P/K	8.9	8.6	8.5	8.3	8.8	9.8	9.0	8.6	9.1	9.5	9.3	8.7	8.6	8.9	8.9	8.0	7.8	8.0	8.1	6.8	5.9	6.1
Australia	P/Y	29.6	30.1	31.7	33.1	34.1	34.5	34.0	34.1	36.1	36.6	36.5	35.9	35.9	36.5	37.1	37.7	35.7	35.3	35.8	33.3	28.9	
Denmark	P/Y	44.2	44.7	46.2	45.2	46.7	47.6	46.7	46.9	46.4	47.7	47.0	46.1	46.6	46.1	45.6	45.0	44.3	45.1	44.6	42.2	41.9	
Netherlands	P/Y	45.4	44.5	43.7	41.8	43.9	44.7	41.6	39.7	37.7	37.5	37.4	36.1	37.4	38.3	38.2	36.7	36.2	37.4	37.2	37.2	34.4	37.3

P = Gross operating surplus. Y = Gross value added. K = Gross capital stock.

TABLE 6.4 NET PROFITS AND RATES OF RETURN: INDUSTRY PLUS TRANSPORT

		1955	1956	1957	1958	1959	1960	1961	1962	1963	1964	1965	1966	1967	1968	1969	1970	1971	1972	1973	1974	1975	1976
Canada	P/Y	31.4	31.9	29.6	28.3	28.9	28.0	28.5	29.3	30.3	31.5	29.9	28.9	27.2	28.3	27.6	26.1	25.8	27.2	29.8	30.0	27.0	26.8
	Y/K	50.2	50.3	46.1	41.3	41.1	39.5	38.7	39.2	39.6	40.7	40.2	40.1	39.0	39.6	38.9	36.5	35.9	36.2	38.9	38.3	34.9	34.9
	P/K	15.8	16.0	13.6	11.7	11.9	11.1	11.0	11.5	12.0	12.8	12.0	11.6	10.6	11.2	10.7	9.5	9.3	9.8	11.6	11.5	9.4	9.3
United States	P/Y	28.6	26.8	26.2	25.2	26.7	26.0	25.9	26.1	26.4	27.0	27.7	27.3	26.1	25.8	24.0	21.9	22.4	22.7	22.3	20.8	23.3	24.2
	Y/K	93.0	89.0	84.3	77.3	83.4	83.5	82.2	85.4	86.6	89.3	90.8	91.0	86.3	85.6	82.4	75.8	73.9	75.6	77.0	73.3	70.6	74.8
	P/K	26.6	23.9	22.1	19.5	22.3	21.7	21.3	22.2	22.9	24.1	25.2	24.8	22.5	22.1	19.8	16.6	16.6	17.2	17.2	15.2	16.5	18.1
Japan	P/Y	31.5	32.5	37.3	34.3	34.4	39.0	39.4	36.4	36.1	35.1	31.7	32.2	34.5	36.6	36.8	36.9	33.9	31.9	28.7	24.9	25.6	
	Y/K	38.6	40.3	43.3	43.5	46.1	51.7	53.3	52.3	53.0	53.9	50.9	51.7	54.4	57.4	57.6	54.7	51.5	47.9	41.0	38.7	40.9	
	P/K	12.2	13.1	16.2	14.9	15.8	20.2	21.0	19.0	19.1	18.9	16.1	16.7	18.8	21.0	21.2	20.1	17.5	15.3	11.8	9.6	10.5	
Germany	P/Y	43.2	42.6	42.6	41.8	42.7	42.4	40.3	38.6	37.6	37.3	37.8	36.9	37.5	38.8	37.7	36.4	35.4	35.0	33.8	33.2	33.0	34.6
	Y/K	89.2	86.5	83.8	80.4	80.1	79.9	76.0	72.1	67.8	67.0	67.8	65.9	62.4	66.3	66.1	66.1	63.5	62.5	63.0	61.6	58.8	60.8
	P/K	38.5	36.9	35.7	33.6	34.2	33.9	30.6	27.9	25.5	25.0	25.6	24.3	23.4	25.8	24.9	24.0	22.5	21.9	21.3	20.4	19.4	21.0
Italy	P/Y	38.7	38.1	38.6	38.8	40.0	39.3	38.6	36.2	31.9	30.6	33.4	34.9	33.0	34.1	34.5	29.7	25.9	26.3				
	Y/K	58.5	57.6	56.2	56.1	58.2	60.6	61.3	61.9	61.3	58.7	57.2	59.2	62.3	60.7	63.2	63.9	58.8	58.4				
	P/K	22.7	21.9	21.7	21.7	23.3	23.8	23.7	22.4	19.5	17.9	19.1	20.7	20.6	20.7	21.8	19.0	15.2	15.3				
Sweden	P/Y	26.9	27.7	28.1	27.7	28.7	27.1	26.1	24.1	22.3	24.0	24.9	22.5	22.4	22.7	24.0	24.4	18.8	19.4	23.8	24.7	16.1	10.2
	Y/K	39.4	38.6	36.7	38.3	37.5	37.2	37.0	37.0	35.3	36.4	37.4	36.5	36.3	36.5	37.1	37.1	33.2	32.8	31.9	31.9	31.2	30.3
	P/K	10.6	10.7	10.9	10.6	10.8	10.1	9.7	8.9	7.9	8.7	9.3	8.2	8.1	8.3	8.9	9.0	6.2	6.3	7.6	7.9	5.0	3.1
United Kingdom	P/Y	23.7	22.5	21.8	21.3	22.5	24.7	22.2	21.0	22.9	23.6	22.7	21.0	21.4	22.5	22.4	19.3	19.2	20.6	20.0	17.1	13.0	14.4
	Y/K	49.1	48.4	47.1	45.4	46.0	48.5	46.9	45.3	45.3	46.5	46.2	44.4	42.4	42.3	41.5	40.1	38.9	38.6	38.4	35.7	34.7	32.9
	P/K	11.6	10.9	10.3	9.7	10.4	12.0	10.4	9.5	10.4	11.0	10.5	9.3	9.1	9.5	9.3	7.8	7.5	7.9	7.7	6.1	4.5	4.7
Australia	P/Y	25.9	26.0	27.3	27.6	28.1	28.4	27.4	27.2	28.9	29.4	29.1	28.1	27.9	28.4	29.2	30.2	28.1	27.6	28.5	26.2	22.1	
Netherlands	P/Y	37.7	36.8	35.9	33.0	35.8	37.3	33.4	31.1	28.9	29.4	29.3	27.8	29.3	30.8	30.6	28.9	27.9	29.0	29.3	29.0	24.8	28.3

P = Net operating surplus. Y = Net value added. K = Net capital stock.

Table 6.5 EXPONENTIAL TRENDS IN FACTOR SHARES AND RATES OF RETURN MANUFACTURING

The levels shown are the expected levels for the final year, 1973 or 1976

	Gross data						Net data					
	Gross Operating Surplus as % of gross value added		Gross Value Added as % of gross capital stock		Gross Operating Surplus as % of gross capital stock		Net Operating Surplus as % of net value added		Net Value Added as % of net capital stock		Net Operating Surplus as % of net capital stock	
	Trend level	% Rate of change	Trend level	% Rate of change	Trend level	% Rate of change	Trend level	% Rate of change	Trend level	% Rate of change	Trend level	% Rate of change
	in 1973		in 1973		in 1973		in 1973		in 1973		in 1973	
1955-1973												
Canada	31.7	−0.63*	41.4	−1.17**	13.2	−1.80**	24.4	−1.21*	61.1	−1.17**	14.9	−2.38**
United States	26.3	−0.10	83.4	0.13	21.9	0.05	20.5	−0.22	143.9	0.09	29.6	−0.13
Japan	48.4	0.06	60.3	0.71	29.2	0.78	37.6	−0.47	64.3	−0.39	24.2	−0.86
Australia	34.2	1.11*					26.5	0.66				
Denmark	40.5	−0.61*										
Germany	30.0	−1.78**	49.3	−0.85**	14.8	−2.63**	21.2	−3.20**	67.2	−0.88*	14.4	−4.03**
Italy[a]	29.3	−2.04**	30.5	0.34	8.9	−1.70*	20.2	−2.54**	48.4	0.55	9.8	−1.99*
Netherlands	33.4	−1.53**					26.9	−1.99**				
Sweden	29.3	−0.41	36.3	−0.60**	10.6	−1.02	22.0	−0.76	49.2	−0.65**	10.8	−1.39
United Kingdom	24.8	−1.77**	34.4	−1.00**	8.5	−2.77**	18.4	−2.78**	49.0	−1.58**	9.0	−4.37**
	in 1976		in 1976		in 1976		in 1976		in 1976		in 1976	
1958-1976												
Canada	32.1	−0.40	41.6	−0.69**	13.3	−1.09*	24.7	−0.79	61.6	−0.64*	15.2	−1.43*
United States	26.3	−0.09	79.2	−0.27	20.9	−0.35	20.3	−0.28	135.6	−0.42	27.5	−0.70
Japan[b]	43.9	−0.95*	52.6	−0.83	23.1	−1.78	32.9	−1.72*	54.0	−2.14*	17.8	−3.86*
Australia[b]	29.9	−0.45					22.9	−0.86				
Denmark[b]	36.7	−1.54**										
Germany	26.9	−2.25**	47.8	−0.87**	12.9	−3.12**	17.2	−4.17**	67.7	−0.50	11.7	−4.64**
Italy[b]	26.3	−2.67**										
Netherlands	33.8	−1.12**					28.1	−1.12*				
Sweden	30.0	−0.10	36.2	−0.48*	10.9	−0.58	22.4	−0.41	48.9	−0.54*	11.0	−0.93
United Kingdom	19.4	−3.37**	29.9	−1.97**	5.8	−5.35**	11.1	−6.23**	43.0	−2.26**	4.8	−8.50**

* $t>3$ ** $t>5$.

a) For Italy, the data run from 1955 to 1972, and the trend levels refer to 1972, not 1973.
b) For these countries, the data run from 1958 to 1975, and the trend levels refer to 1975, not 1976.

TABLE 6.6 EXPONENTIAL TRENDS IN FACTOR SHARES AND RATES OF RETURN INDUSTRY PLUS TRANSPORT

The levels shown are the expected levels for the final year: 1973 or 1976

	Gross data						Net data					
	Gross Operating Surplus as % of gross value added		Gross Value Added as % of gross capital stock		Gross Operating Surplus as % of gross capital stock		Net Operating Surplus as % of net value added		Net Value Added as % of net capital stock		Net Operating Surplus as % of net capital stock	
	Trend level	% Rate of change	Trend level	% Rate of change	Trend level	% Rate of change	Trend level	% Rate of change	Trend level	% Rate of change	Trend level	% Rate of change
	in 1973		in 1973		in 1973		in 1973		in 1973		in 1973	
1955-1973												
Canada	36.3	−0.22	27.0	−0.83*	9.8	−1.04*	27.2	−0.62*	35.9	−1.33**	9.8	−1.97*
United States[a]	31.4	−0.62**	51.9	−0.15	16.3	−0.77	23.2	−1.04*	78.9	−0.65	18.3	−1.68*
Japan	46.2	0.19	51.9	2.15**	24.0	2.34*	33.6	−0.33	54.2	1.06	18.2	0.73
Australia	37.8	0.97**					29.1	0.42*				
Denmark	45.6	−0.08										
Germany	41.4	−0.75**	45.5	−0.89**	18.9	−1.63**	35.5	−1.04**	59.7	−1.99**	20.7	−3.25**
Italy[b]	34.6	−1.83**	40.8	0.55*	14.3	−1.39*	28.1	−2.12**	61.6	0.35	17.3	−1.77*
Netherlands	35.4	−1.25**					27.4	−1.56**				
Sweden	30.2	−0.95**	27.5	−0.73**	8.3	−1.67**	20.9	−1.69**	34.0	−0.75*	7.1	−2.54**
United Kingdom	29.9	−0.02	27.9	−0.42	8.3	−0.47	20.4	−0.74*	39.2	−1.31**	8.0	−2.06**
	in 1976		in 1976		in 1976		in 1976		in 1976		in 1976	
1958-1976												
Canada	36.4	−0.12	27.0	−0.48	9.9	−0.57	27.5	−0.36	36.1	−0.74**	9.9	−1.12*
United States[a]	30.8	−0.66**	49.4	−0.47	15.2	−1.14*	22.4	−1.09*	75.0	−0.86*	16.8	−1.95*
Japan[c]	42.1	−0.76	46.4	0.60	19.6	−0.15	29.2	−1.64*	46.7	−0.73	13.6	−2.35
Australia[c]	34.7	−0.10					26.8	−0.44				
Denmark[c]	43.6	−0.52*										
Germany	40.5	−0.74**	43.4	−1.14**	17.6	−1.87**	33.9	−1.13**	58.6	−1.58**	19.5	−2.86**
Italy[c]	31.3	−2.47**										
Netherlands	35.3	−0.94**					26.8	−1.27*				
Sweden	27.9	−1.38*	26.1	−0.98**	7.3	−2.34**	17.2	−2.91*	31.9	−1.11**	5.5	−4.05**
United Kingdom	27.9	−0.58	25.1	−1.26**	7.0	−1.88	16.7	−2.19*	35.4	−1.86**	5.9	−4.08**

* $t>3$ ** $t>5$.

a) The U.S. data include distribution and miscellaneous services.
b) The data for Italy run from 1955 to 1972, and the trend levels refer to 1972, not 1973.
c) The data for these countries run from 1958 to 1975, and the trend levels refer to 1975 not 1976.

Diagram 6.1

MANUFACTURING

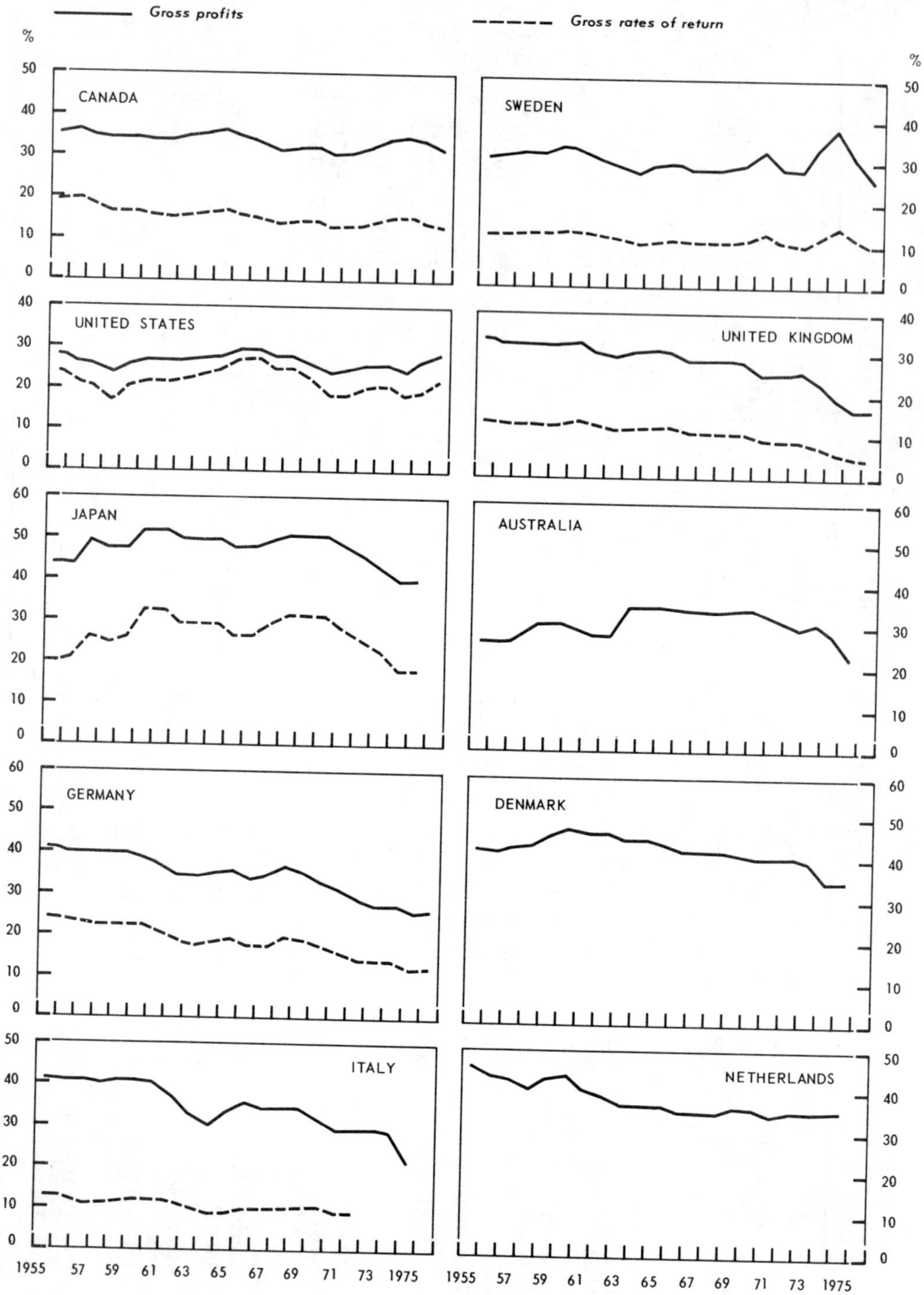

Diagram 6.2
MANUFACTURING

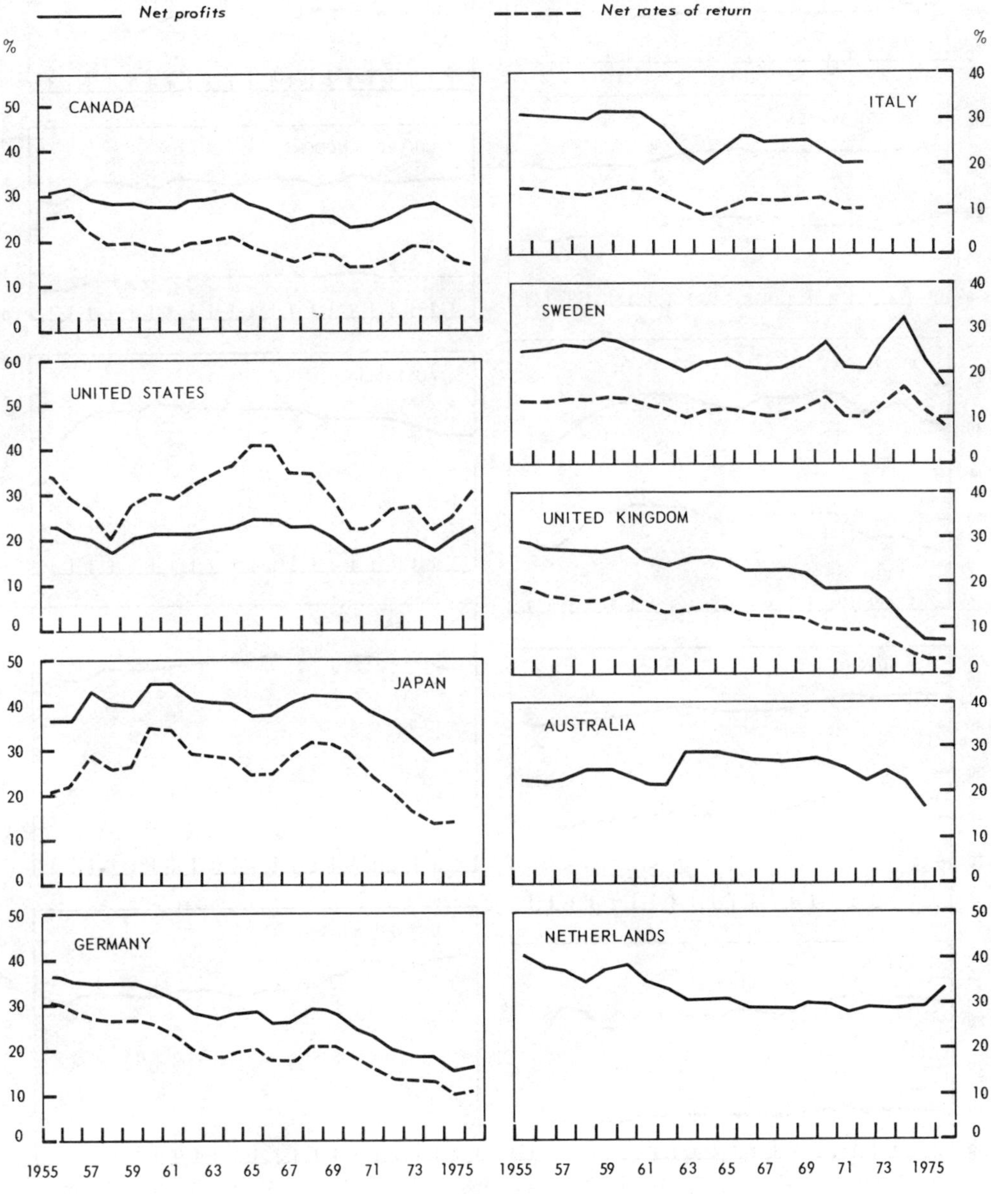

Diagram 6.3

INDUSTRY AND TRANSPORT

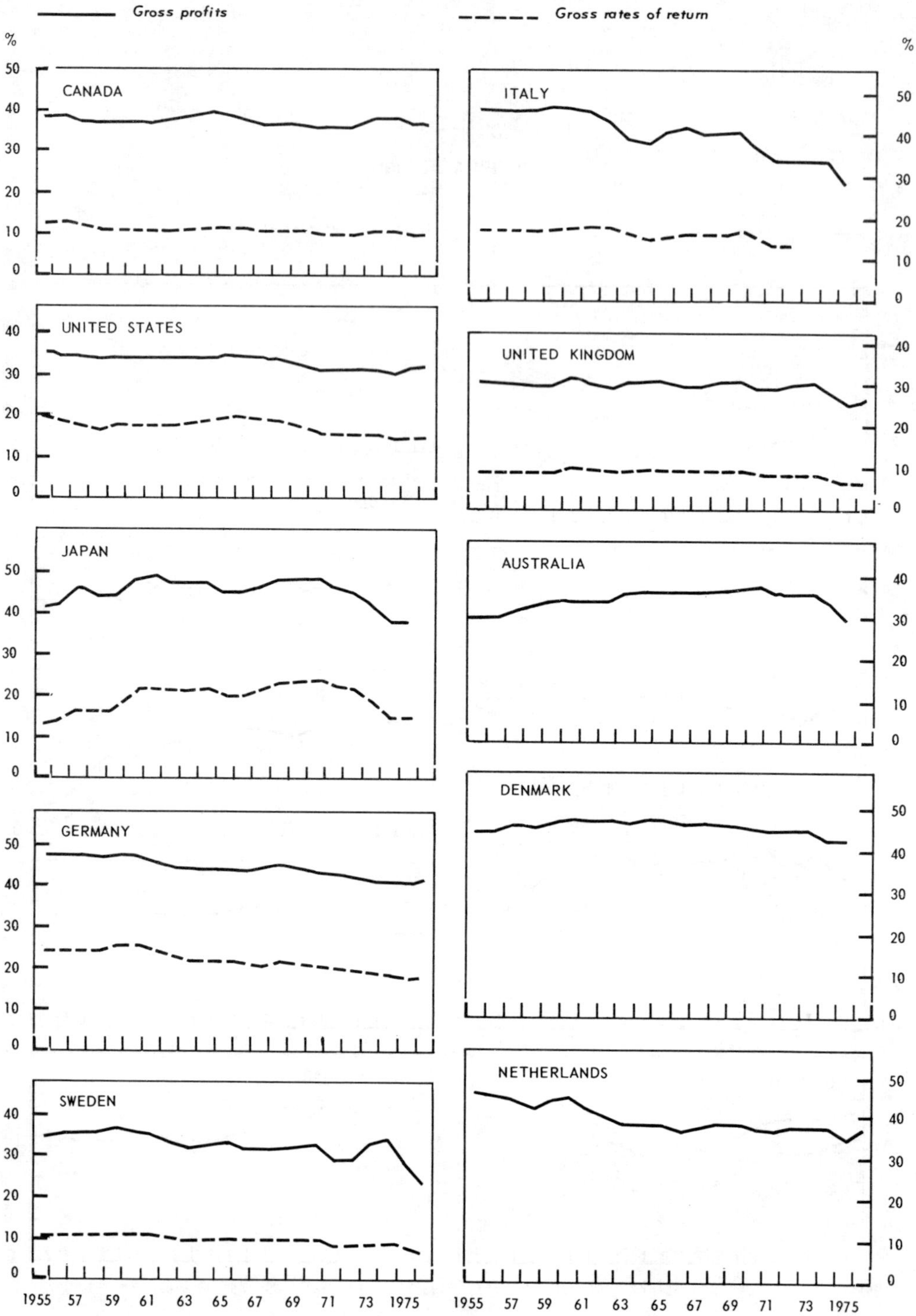

Diagram 6.4

INDUSTRY AND TRANSPORT

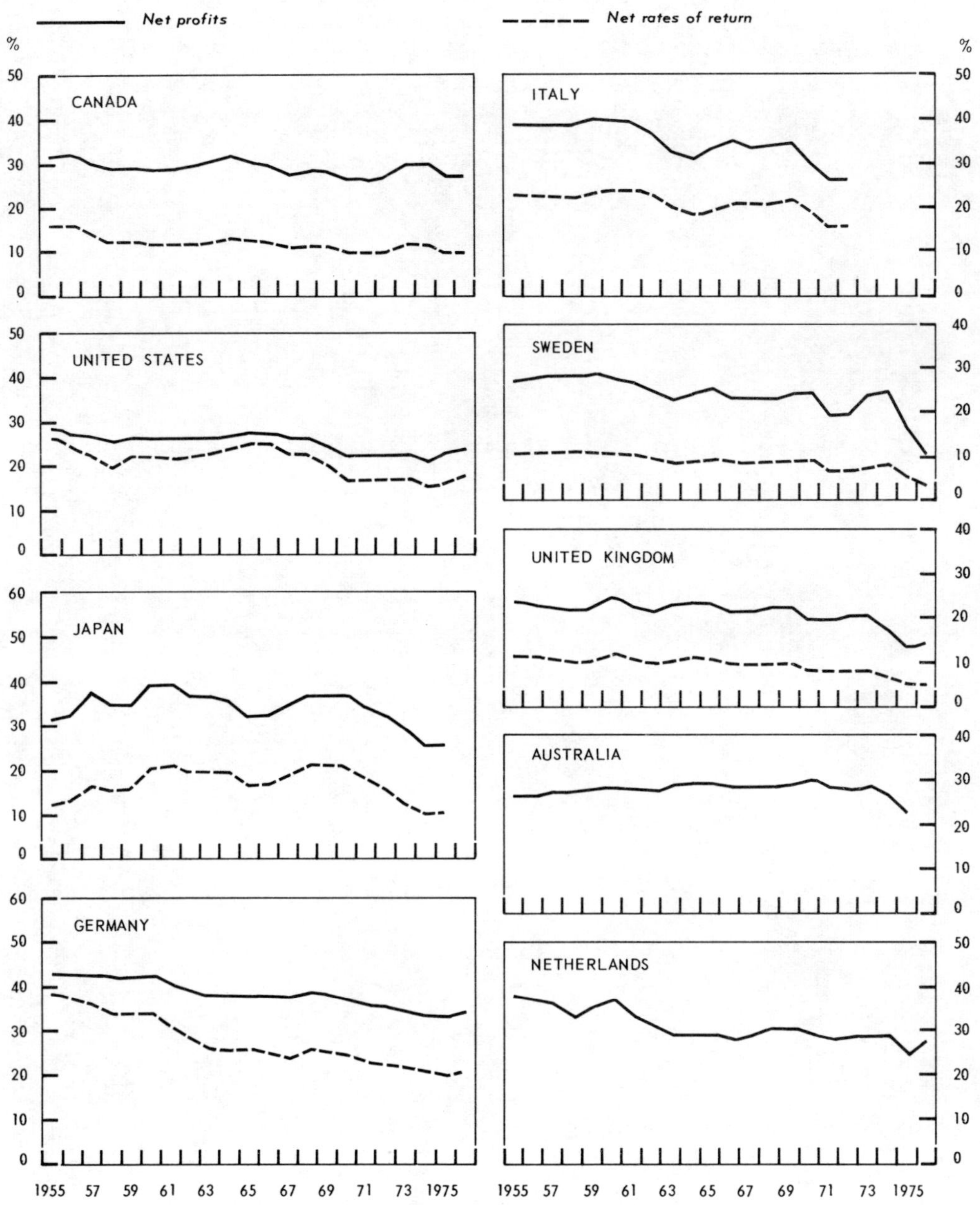

Appendix

STATISTICAL SOURCES

The data on value added and the operating surplus used in this chapter were, so far as possible, taken directly from the National Accounts questionnaires returned to the OECD by individual member countries. Where appropriate, these data have already been adjusted by national statistical offices to bring them into line with SNA concepts and definitions. Most, but not all, of these data are published by the OECD in their National Accounts Yearbooks. In addition, however, it was usually necessary to refer back to the National Accounts publications of the individual countries, either to obtain data classified in greater detail or data for earlier years than those covered by the questionnaires.

The following is a list of national publications used for each country to complement the OECD data and to obtain data on capital stock which are not part of the National Accounts questionnaire.

CANADA

National Income and Expenditure Accounts 1961-1975, Statistics Canada, Ottawa.

Fixed Capital Flows and Stocks 1929-1973 and 1974-1975, Statistics Canada, Ottawa.

UNITED STATES

Survey of Current Business, July 1976, Department of Commerce, Washington, D.C.

Supplement to the Survey of Current Business 1929-1974, Department of Commerce, Washington D.C.

JAPAN

Annual Report on National Income Statistics, 1976 and 1977, Economic Planning Agency, Tokyo.

Estimates of the Stock of Non-residential Business Capital, Economic Planning Agency, Tokyo.

Social Overhead Capital (Confidential), Economic Planning Agency, Tokyo.

GERMANY

Volkswirtschaftliche Gesamtrechnungen, Fachserie 18 : *Reihe 1 Konten und Standardtabellen, 1975.*

Reihe S2, Revidierte Ergebnisse, 1960-1976, Statistisches Bundesamt, Wiesbaden.

ITALY

Annuario di Contabilità Nazionale, Vol. V, 1975, Tomo I, Istituto Centrale di Statistica, Rome.

Conti Nazionali, 1973, Istituto Centrale di Statistica, Rome.

Il Capitale Fisso Riproducible Delle Attività Industriali, Anni 1951-1972, Istituto Centrale di Statistica, March 1975, Rome.

Lo Sviluppo Economico in Italia, Vol. III, Giorgio Ferà (ed) 1969, Milan.

SWEDEN

Statistiska Meddelanden, N 1976: 7.4 Nationalrakenskaper 1963-1975, Central Bureau of Statistics, Stockholm.

Statistiska Meddelanden, N 1975: 98, Appendix 2 Capital Formation, Repair and Maintenance and Stocks of Fixed Capital, Central Bureau of Statistics, Stockholm.

UNITED KINGDOM

National Income and Expenditure, 1965-1975, Central Statistical Office, London.

AUSTRALIA

National Income and Expenditure, 1973-1974, 1974-1975, Australian Bureau of Statistics, Canberra.

DENMARK

Statistiske Efterretninger A 1976: 36, 68 Årgang, Danmarks Statistik, Copenhagen.

NETHERLANDS

Nationale Rekeningen 1973, Central Bureau of Statistics, The Hague.

National Accounts, ESA, 1970-1975, Eurostat, 1976.

OECD SALES AGENTS
DÉPOSITAIRES DES PUBLICATIONS DE L'OCDE

ARGENTINA – ARGENTINE
Carlos Hirsch S.R.L., Florida 165,
BUENOS-AIRES, Tel. 33-1787-2391 Y 30-7122

AUSTRALIA – AUSTRALIE
Australia & New Zealand Book Company Pty Ltd.,
23 Cross Street, (P.O.B. 459)
BROOKVALE NSW 2100 Tel. 938-2244

AUSTRIA – AUTRICHE
Gerold and Co., Graben 31, WIEN 1. Tel. 52.22.35

BELGIUM – BELGIQUE
LCLS
44 rue Otlet, B1070 BRUXELLES. Tel. 02-521 28 13

BRAZIL – BRÉSIL
Mestre Jou S.A., Rua Guaipà 518,
Caixa Postal 24090, 05089 SAO PAULO 10. Tel. 261-1920
Rua Senador Dantas 19 s/205-6, RIO DE JANEIRO GB.
Tel. 232-07. 32

CANADA
Renouf Publishing Company Limited,
2182 St. Catherine Street West,
MONTREAL, Quebec H3H 1M7 Tel. (514) 937-3519

DENMARK – DANEMARK
Munksgaards Boghandel,
Nørregade 6, 1165 KØBENHAVN K. Tel. (01) 12 85 70

FINLAND – FINLANDE
Akateeminen Kirjakauppa
Keskuskatu 1, 00100 HELSINKI 10. Tel. 625.901

FRANCE
Bureau des Publications de l'OCDE,
2 rue André-Pascal, 75775 PARIS CEDEX 16. Tel. (1) 524.81.67
Principal correspondant :
13602 AIX-EN-PROVENCE : Librairie de l'Université.
Tel. 26.18.08

GERMANY – ALLEMAGNE
Alexander Horn,
D - 6200 WIESBADEN, Spiegelgasse 9
Tel. (6121) 37-42-12

GREECE – GRÈCE
Librairie Kauffmann, 28 rue du Stade,
ATHÈNES 132. Tel. 322.21.60

HONG-KONG
Government Information Services,
Sales and Publications Office, Beaconsfield House, 1st floor,
Queen's Road, Central. Tel. H-233191

ICELAND – ISLANDE
Snaebjörn Jónsson and Co., h.f.,
Hafnarstraeti 4 and 9, P.O.B. 1131, REYKJAVIK.
Tel. 13133/14281/11936

INDIA – INDE
Oxford Book and Stationery Co.:
NEW DELHI, Scindia House. Tel. 45896
CALCUTTA, 17 Park Street. Tel. 240832

ITALY – ITALIE
Libreria Commissionaria Sansoni:
Via Lamarmora 45, 50121 FIRENZE. Tel. 579751
Via Bartolini 29, 20155 MILANO. Tel. 365083
Sub-depositari:
Editrice e Libreria Herder,
Piazza Montecitorio 120, 00 186 ROMA. Tel. 674628
Libreria Hoepli, Via Hoepli 5, 20121 MILANO. Tel. 865446
Libreria Lattes, Via Garibaldi 3, 10122 TORINO. Tel. 519274
La diffusione delle edizioni OCSE è inoltre assicurata dalle migliori librerie nelle città più importanti.

JAPAN – JAPON
OECD Publications and Information Center
Akasaka Park Building, 2-3-4 Akasaka, Minato-ku,
TOKYO 107. Tel. 586-2016

KOREA - CORÉE
Pan Korea Book Corporation,
P.O.Box n° 101 Kwangwhamun, SÉOUL. Tel. 72-7369

LEBANON – LIBAN
Documenta Scientifica/Redico,
Edison Building, Bliss Street, P.O.Box 5641, BEIRUT.
Tel. 354429–344425

MEXICO & CENTRAL AMERICA
Centro de Publicaciones de Organismos Internacionales S.A.,
Alfonso Herrera N° 72, 1er Piso,
Apdo. Postal 42-051, MEXICO 4 D.F.

THE NETHERLANDS – PAYS-BAS
Staatsuitgeverij
Chr. Plantijnstraat
'S-GRAVENHAGE. Tel. 070-814511
Voor bestellingen: Tel. 070-624551

NEW ZEALAND – NOUVELLE-ZÉLANDE
The Publications Manager,
Government Printing Office,
WELLINGTON: Mulgrave Street (Private Bag),
World Trade Centre, Cubacade, Cuba Street,
Rutherford House, Lambton Quay, Tel. 737-320
AUCKLAND: Rutland Street (P.O.Box 5344), Tel. 32.919
CHRISTCHURCH: 130 Oxford Tce (Private Bag), Tel. 50.331
HAMILTON: Barton Street (P.O.Box 857), Tel. 80.103
DUNEDIN: T & G Building, Princes Street (P.O.Box 1104),
Tel. 78.294

NORWAY – NORVÈGE
J.G. TANUM A/S,
P.O. Box 1177 Sentrum, OSLO 1

PAKISTAN
Mirza Book Agency, 65 Shahrah Quaid-E-Azam, LAHORE 3.
Tel. 66839

PORTUGAL
Livraria Portugal, Rua do Carmo 70-74,
1117 LISBOA CODEX.
Tel. 360582/3

SPAIN – ESPAGNE
Mundi-Prensa Libros, S.A.
Castelló 37, Apartado 1223, MADRID-1. Tel. 275.46.55
Libreria Bastinos, Pelayo, 52, BARCELONA 1. Tel. 222.06.00

SWEDEN – SUÈDE
AB CE Fritzes Kungl Hovbokhandel,
Box 16 356, S 103 27 STH, Regeringsgatan 12,
DS STOCKHOLM. Tel. 08/23 89 00

SWITZERLAND – SUISSE
Librairie Payot, 6 rue Grenus, 1211 GENÈVE 11. Tel. 022-31.89.50

TAIWAN – FORMOSE
National Book Company,
84-5 Sing Sung Rd., Sec. 3, TAIPEI 107. Tel. 321.0698

UNITED KINGDOM – ROYAUME-UNI
H.M. Stationery Office, P.O.B. 569,
LONDON SE1 9 NH. Tel. 01-928-6977, Ext. 410 or
49 High Holborn, LONDON WC1V 6 HB (personal callers)
Branches at: EDINBURGH, BIRMINGHAM, BRISTOL,
MANCHESTER, CARDIFF, BELFAST.

UNITED STATES OF AMERICA
OECD Publications and Information Center, Suite 1207,
1750 Pennsylvania Ave., N.W. WASHINGTON, D.C.20006.
Tel. (202)724-1857

VENEZUELA
Libreria del Este, Avda. F. Miranda 52, Edificio Galipán,
CARACAS 106. Tel. 32 23 01/33 26 04/33 24 73

YUGOSLAVIA – YOUGOSLAVIE
Jugoslovenska Knjiga, Terazije 27, P.O.B. 36, BEOGRAD.
Tel. 621-992

Les commandes provenant de pays où l'OCDE n'a pas encore désigné de dépositaire peuvent être adressées à :
OCDE, Bureau des Publications, 2 rue André-Pascal, 75775 PARIS CEDEX 16.
Orders and inquiries from countries where sales agents have not yet been appointed may be sent to:
OECD, Publications Office, 2 rue André-Pascal, 75775 PARIS CEDEX 16.

OECD PUBLICATIONS, 2 rue André-Pascal, 75775 Paris Cedex 16 - No. 40 951 1979
PRINTED IN FRANCE
(11 79 02 1) ISBN 92-64-21917-X